Wrap It Up!

Wrap It Up!

Creative Gift Wrapping for All Occasions

Ruth J. Katz

ILLUSTRATIONS BY JUDY TONELLI

Color Photography by The Ernest Silva Studio, New York City
Styling Assistance by Rowann Gilman

DOUBLEDAY & COMPANY, INC.   GARDEN CITY, NEW YORK

The author is grateful to the following companies for their generous contribution to this book. Their charming, festive, and gay wrapping supplies, papers, and ribbons are responsible for most of the wrappings that appear on the following pages.

Woven edge ribbons courtesy of C. M. Offray & Son
Cut edge ribbons courtesy of Lion Ribbon Company
Assorted gift wrapping novelties courtesy of Dennison
   Stationery Products
Gift wrapping papers courtesy of Hallmark Cards, Inc., Family Line, Inc., and Finch Handprints (a division of C. R. Gibson Company)

Library of Congress Cataloging in Publication Data

Katz, Ruth J.
  Wrap it up!

   1. Gift wrapping. I. Title.
TT870.K288 1983   745.54
ISBN: 0-385-18519-7
Library of Congress Catalog Card Number 81-43574

Printed in the United States of America

Design by Jeanette Portelli

This one is for my parents, dearer to me than I can express.
Thank you both for all that you have done.

Acknowledgments

I want to thank my family and friends for once more tolerating yet another book. I'm certain that my litany of "I can't; I have to work on my book" has not only worn thin but has also become rather tedious over the years. So, an enormous thank you to my parents and my dear friends Julie and the two Karens who have repeatedly heard the same lamentable story and politely listened to my travails for so long.

I lovingly thank my illustrator Judy Tonelli for all her energy, enthusiasm (even when mine was lacking), and ability to creatively visualize my verbal meanderings, without benefit of Polaroid. Her imaginative, charming, and clear illustrations make me love this book all the more. Bless you, Judy.

What can I say to sweet, tireless Robin Weiss? This book wouldn't have half its verve without her cunning, sparkling ideas and nimble fingers.

To Rowann Gilman, my friend who helped me with all those "bunnies changing hands," a round of applause for rallying to my needs at the photo studio and for always locating just the right "little stuff" to embellish a shot. And, of course, a deep bow to the professional staff at the Silva Studio and to the delightful Alex Gotfryd for his readiness to photograph me—and to retain the "plastic surgeon" for my vanity.

Very special thanks are in order for my two editors, Marlene Connor and Mary Sherwin. Marlene was as sympathetic, thoughtful, and constructive an editor as one could want, always bestowing her wisdom with humor. Mary, who inherited me midstream, deserves much credit for her insightful and clever suggestions, prudent editing, and patience.

Also, I cannot forget Carol Floriani, who really made this whole thing happen. Thank you.

Contents

Three   The Basics of Wrapping 41

Wrap It Up!

CHAPTER ONE

A Brief History of Gift Wrapping

*E*veryone likes to receive presents. And when you get a present that is beautifully wrapped it makes you feel that much more special.

A gift is twice as sweet when love and care have gone into its presentation. Of course, not every present *must* be wrapped extravagantly. As you will see in subsequent chapters, there are many creative ways to use odds and ends to wrap your presents, without sacrificing beauty. In fact everyday items can be used to make the wrappings look quite spectacular. You will be able to do a great deal with a small amount of money, a little bit of effort, and a larger amount of imagination!

People have been giving each other gifts for centuries. The use of decorated, embellished packages to contain gifts is an old custom, developed over time by various cultures. Even in the Bible it is said that the Wise Men gave the newborn Christ Child gifts of gold, frankincense, and myrrh, which they probably presented in beautiful containers.

In ancient times, the Chinese decorated their presents with beautiful, shimmering, tinsel-like ribbons and often wrapped them in parchment papers. German toymakers wrapped their manufactured products in gaily colored papers (roughly akin to our bookbinding papers), in an effort to avoid paying duty when they shipped these goods abroad. It is said that when German toys reached England, the bookbinders there smoothed out the crumpled marbleized papers and used them for their own craft.

The English are also partly responsible for today's use of gift wrap paper, as they were the first people to make wallpaper in the early sixteenth century. Wallpaper was also used generously to wrap packages, and although it was not specifically created for that purpose, the idea caught on. White tissue paper was born, colored cordings were added, and presto!—wrapped boxes! The dressed-up package was definitely on its way to making an appearance at every holiday by the beginning of this century.

In 1901 the first commercial gift tags were produced in the United States, followed soon after by gummed decorative labels. Although the designs that were used—holly leaves, to be precise— were not that innovative, they sold extremely well. People used many gummed stickers to decorate plain tissue paper, and then the inevitable happened—printed tissue paper made its debut in the marketplace, decorated (as might be suspected) with holly leaves. The holly leaf pattern was so popular, in fact, that one manufacturer had holly leaf tissue paper in his line for fifteen years before the public demanded other designs.

The Hallmark Company, a pioneer in the gift wrapping industry, made great strides in the 1920s in producing and importing assorted wrappings, ribbons, and decorative tinsels. In 1930 they produced wonderful ribbon that sticks to itself when moistened.

In 1931, a resourceful manufacturer invented curling or crimping ribbon, a product that can make even the plainest brown wrapping paper look jolly.

Surprisingly, gift wrapping remained highly popular throughout the Depression. It probably helped to lighten spirits, which was well worth the extra pennies.

Today, people all around the world have their own gift wrapping customs. Ask a friend from abroad how people in his/her country wrap gifts. You may learn some new tricks. For example:

• In Africa, gifts are wrapped in colors that represent the giver's feelings toward the recipient. Red cloth symbolizes wishes for health, while grass or any type of foliage indicates hopes for wealth.

• Whereas in the United States blue paper is traditionally used to wrap gifts for a baby boy and pink paper for a baby girl, in Belgium, the opposite color arrangement is used.

• In parts of Germany packages are wrapped in a fashion that we would call "inside out." The plain, ordinary side of the paper is put on the outside, while the decorative, fancy side of the paper goes on the inside. This creates a double surprise on the inside, since the recipient has no idea what the paper looks like until he or she starts to open the package.

• Another interesting custom, which is also a noteworthy footnote to the history of gift wrapping, is from the archives of the Gift Wrapping & Tyings Association of America. They tell us that in recent years, manufacturers noticed that they were selling a fair amount of Santa Claus-imprinted Christmas wrapping paper to people living in the South Pacific. It was particularly unusual that the sales were made in August, not in December. Upon further investigation, the manufacturers learned that the natives in those lands believed that Santa Claus was a deity and his beloved Dasher, Dancer, Prancer, Vixen, Comet, Cupid, Donner, and Blitzen were fates. The islanders were buying the paper in quantities large enough to paper the walls of their homes to ensure safety from visits by evil spirits. (This is an ironic corollary to the invention by the English of wallpaper, which they used to beautify walls and later to decorate gift boxes. In the South Sea Islands, the reverse has taken place: gift wrapping paper is now being put up on walls!)

No matter what the history, the custom, or the wrapping style, beautifully garnished packages are a joy. Even if you *hate* to wrap a package, you can still present your gift artistically with a minimum of effort. For example, a glossy, bright-colored shopping bag with a big bow tied around the handles provides an instant wrapping. Or, you can decorate a box, using miscellaneous trinkets you'll find in some of your drawers at home. A dash of inspiration, a dollop of ribbons, a spray of paint, and an ounce of determination will take you a long way.

CHAPTER TWO

Supplies and Equipment

*P*apers suitable for gift wrapping aren't sold only in stationery, party-goods, or department stores. An industrial plastics shop, for example, will stock all types of vinyls, bubble wrap, colored mylar sheets, plastic gels, and a veritable cornucopia of inexpensive plastic objects. An industrial paper plant or a printing factory would be an excellent source for all types of unusual papers. Soft corrugated cardboard used for packing is great for wrapping oddly shaped gifts. Keep on the lookout while you do your shopping for other possibilities to wrap your gifts.

Yarn and knitting shops stock hundreds of varieties of novelty filaments, Lurex threads, and thick, ropelike fibers, as well as traditional yarns. Discount stores sell many varieties of string, jute, sisal, hemp, and even clothesline. These all take dye well; so if you find yourself with nothing to do on a rainy afternoon, make a dye bath for a dozen balls of string. Be inventive with color.

PAPERS

Standard Gift Wrapping Papers

These papers come in many varieties. You can buy them in folded packages or rolled on long cardboard tubes. There are stripes, prints, paisleys, swirls, tiny Victorian-looking floral motifs, bold graphics, geometrics, checks, plaids, and even mundane solids. You can also choose between high-gloss and matte finishes, and metallic surfaces that practically reflect your image like a mirror.

This kind of paper is available in an endless variety of colors, including pastels; sophisticated shades; rich-looking, silk-screened tones; and somber, no-nonsense hues. Surface finishes range from grainy and textured, to smooth, to embossed or raised. There are even reversible wraps, as well as elegantly printed Japanese rice papers. In short, there is no end to what is on the market. Seek and ye shall find.

Tissue Paper

This is the second most popular paper for gift wrapping. It is available in a broad spectrum of colors, prints, and tones. The surface of the paper may be glazed or matte. There are a few different grades or qualities of tissue paper on the market and some are not color-fast. If you have to apply water to tissue paper —in order to dye it, for instance—test a sample of the paper first to see whether it meets your needs.

You can use solid-colored tissue paper to make printed wrapping paper by dipping it in water and dyes. Here's how:

Batik-Style Dyed Tissue Paper

Materials:
1 package (usually ten sheets, measuring 20 × 30 inches) tissue paper (colored tissue paper may be used, but the technique should first be mastered with *white* paper, which gives more visible results)

Small glass bowls, one for each color (of paint or food coloring)
White paper towels
Watercolor or acrylic paints or food coloring; assorted colors
Blotting paper or newspaper

To dye the tissue paper:

1. Fold one sheet of paper in accordion folds, across its length, so that you end up with a piece of paper about 4 inches wide and 20 inches long.
2. Make accordion folds in the opposite direction, also folding the 20-inch measurement down to about 4 inches. You will finish with a small, thick 4-inch square of tissue paper.
3. Immerse the entire piece of folded paper in a shallow bowl of lukewarm water. Use the bathroom sink, if possible. Do not immerse the paper for very long; it will quickly absorb water.
4. Quickly blot the paper between clean paper towels.
5. Fill the small glass bowls with water and add some paint or food coloring to each. The finished color on the tissue paper will be lighter than the color in the bowls, so make the color in the dye baths deeper than you think you want.
6. Take the folded piece of tissue paper and dip different parts of it into each dye bath. For example, dip one corner of the tissue paper into one bath, another corner into another bath, or one entire edge in a particular dye bath. After each dipping, blot the tissue paper very well, pressing out all excessive moisture between the paper towels and newspaper. Allow to dry for a few hours.
7. When the tissue paper is still slightly damp, carefully open up the accordion pleats, in the reverse order from which you made them. You will get a colorful batiklike or tie-dyed-looking piece of gift wrapping paper. Spread it open on paper towels under which you have laid a solid layer of newspaper. Then cover it with another layer of paper towels and more newspaper. Allow to dry—outdoors, if possible. You can even use an iron set at a very low temperature carefully over the entire assembly.

After your first experiment with the above method, you will quickly learn just how much water the tissue paper you have selected can take. You may also wish to use a color of paper other than white as the ground or main surface.

Another way to make printed gift wrap paper on a solid color involves a printing method most of us learned in grade school. But just because it was learned then doesn't mean that it should be dismissed as too unsophisticated for our needs now. Many of us learned this method as linoleum block printing, or vegetable or eraser printing. Vegetable printing is, to my mind, the easiest and most versatile technique. This is a great rainy-day project to do with children.

Vegetable Printing on Solid Tissue Paper

(*Note:* This method of decoration can be used with other types of papers, such as newsprint or brown kraft paper.)

Materials:
Assorted vegetables and fruits; for starters, a green pepper, a large whole carrot, a potato, and a small apple
Small paring knife
Aluminum foil, or several small pie (or tart) tins
Assorted bright colors of acrylic paints (preferably in tubes, as they are the thickest paints); printing inks are also usable
1 package of white tissue paper, as described in the Batik-Style section
Blotting paper or newspaper
Paper towels (white, so that the dyes will not come off on your work)

To print the tissue paper (with the pepper and carrot, first):

1. Cut each vegetable in half. Cut the carrot in half across its length so that you have half of it with a smooth, knife-cut edge. You may cut on a slant for variety. Cut the pepper in half lengthwise. It is not necessary to clean out the inside, as the solid part of the interior "meat" as well as the seeds will provide interest to your design.

2. Use the small aluminum pie tins or pieces of foil to hold individual color paints. Squeeze the paint from the tube and "mush" around with the cut edge of the carrot, using it like a pestle. The paint should be spread out on the flat surface evenly.

3. Dab the flat, paint-covered surface of the carrot on the tissue paper and see what you get. Continue to imprint the carrot's design until it is free from paint. Notice that the color gets fainter and fainter as you work, since you are depositing its paint supply on the paper. Determine the color level you like and try to achieve it again. After you develop some expertise using the carrot, switch to the pepper.

4. Place the cut edge of the pepper in another plate of paint and move it around to evenly absorb the paint. Then press it onto the tissue paper. With all the vegetables, use some scrap paper to print the first sample of each new color, so that you can see what you are going to get before working on your "good" paper. Work on a flat surface (layered with newspaper) so that the printing is neat and uncomplicated. Notice the interesting shape you get from the pepper—particularly from the seeds.

5. When you are more comfortable with this technique, plan a sheet of gift wrap paper that is more elaborately designed than a helter-skelter random stamping of vegetables. Perhaps do horizontal lines, diagonal lines, circles, intersecting stripes, or small waves.

6. When the entire sheet of tissue paper is printed, blot carefully with paper towels, if necessary. If the sheet is still wet with ink, blot additionally with newspaper and allow to dry thoroughly before using or putting away.

To print tissue paper with the potato:

The potato is more challenging for vegetable printing than the carrot and the pepper, which have interesting shapes, grains, or textures. The potato has a wide, smooth surface that can be carved with a paring knife.

(*Note:* Don't allow small children to work unsupervised with this technique; work with them to do the cutting, and then they can proceed alone to do the printing.)

1. Draw (or incise into the potato's cut, flat surface) a pattern that you wish to make. For simplicity's sake, let's use a star here. Draw the star shape in the center of the potato. Then, cut out the shape, going about ½ inch deep, and remove all the rest of the potato around it.

2. Press the potato into the paint or ink, as with the carrot or pepper. Notice, however, that the only part of the potato that takes the paint is the raised star design. Print with the potato and all you get is a star! This is a very different effect from the circular grain of the carrot.

3. Return to the other half of the potato and draw the same star in the center. This time, *do not* cut away the exterior of the design; instead, cut away the interior. That is, cut the star outline and then dig out the star shape, going down about ½ inch. Now print with the potato and what do you get? A potato shape with a white star in the center.

4. Finish the gift wrap paper as you completed it with the pepper or carrot.

As for working with an apple, you can cut it in half, down the core, and print with it. Or you can use a section of the apple and cut it out as you did with the potato. Other interesting vegetables to work with in vegetable printing include a head of lettuce or cabbage (the grainy, circuitous lines of the leaves make beautiful patterns on the paper); an onion, with its elegant concentric circles; and a celery stalk, to make pretty half-moon shapes. Experiment with whatever is in the vegetable bin.

EMBELLISHED TISSUE PAPER is one of the most useful and versatile of all the papers on the market. It's perfect for padding, packing, and filling in holes—like the times when you have to put a round gift in a square box. Or it can be crumpled into soft balls to make comfortable beds for delicate presents. Tissue paper is also reusable. You can get wrinkles out by ironing the paper.

Crepe Paper

Crepe paper is an item that you will undoubtedly use a good deal in your gift wrapping. It is similar to tissue paper, but is finely grained, wrinkled, and usually a heavier weight. The wrinkles are achieved in the manufacturing process, by passing the still wet paper through rollers, thereby compressing it. Because it has those crimps, crepe paper will stretch, which makes it ideal for scalloped and frilly trims. Once stretched, however, it is not resilient enough to return to its original form. So, don't make a mistake when you are working with crepe paper in a stretched-pattern design.

Different brands of crepe paper are available, and their quality varies. The best quality is the type that is most flexible and has a sharp color. There is a wide selection of bright, tempting colors from which to choose. If you are going to work with your crepe paper near water, test it for color-fastness.

Years ago, a two-toned crepe paper was available, with one side of the paper one color, and the other side of the paper another color. It made an ideal paper for gift wrapping novelties, decorations, and party favors. Regrettably, that paper is no longer commercially available. However, if you desire the look of two-toned paper, work with two sheets of different colored paper, back to back, and treat them as if they were one.

Papers from the Art Supply Store

COLOR AID PAPER comes in a seemingly infinite number of shades, and every color has a rich depth to it. ARTISTS' PANTONE PAPERS are available in a wide range of tones and hues that will make it difficult for you to determine just *which* dusty rose is the *right* dusty rose for the package you want to wrap. Both of these papers are costly, so save them for special effects on packages that require only a small amount of paper, as a design, collage, or appliqué on the box. They are delicate papers to work with and mar easily from fingerprints. Furthermore, they cannot be manipulated as easily as gift wrapping paper, so they are not really suitable for wrapping an entire package. But, for those occasions when you want unusual color effects, you will find no better group of papers.

FLINT PAPERS are thin, high-gloss, lustrous papers, which are available by the large sheet, like the two types of papers above. They come in about seventy colors and are easier to work with, as they fold more easily and make relatively neat corners.

MALLEABLE CORK is available in processed sheets that are supple enough to wrap around a container; some even come in different cork colorations.

FINE WRITING AND DRAWING PAPERS, including heavy, beautifully processed vellums, parchments, rice papers, and even handmade papers, are all lovely wrapping choices.

FRAMING PAPERS, which are generally too heavy for gift wrapping, may work for a particular project that needs the protection of a heavy, colored board. Ask about gold and silver Bainbridge Board, used as mattes in framing. Most Bainbridge Board is heavy, but the shiny gold and silver are lighter in weight and very pretty.

PLASTIC FILMS AND SHEETS OF SHEER PLASTIC—clear and in colors—are not necessarily meant for gift wrapping, but may be just what you want for a specific gift, especially one with an odd shape, since plastic wrapping is quite malleable.

MARBLEIZED PAPERS were originally developed for the book-binding industry, but you can now find a gift wrapping paper that resembles the original. Specialty stores and art supply stores have sheets of the heavier marbleized and bookbinding papers. These papers make smart, sophisticated wrappings, and are generally strong enough to be used again. The colors on marbleized papers are usually so luxurious that a bow might detract from the elegance of the paper.

If you fail to find marbleized and bookbinding papers in your local stores, you can make your own.

Materials:
Large, shallow plastic tray (something you don't mind getting dirty)
Newspaper
Several cans of oil-based spray paint, colors as desired
Good-quality watercolor paper (however, marbleizing can be done on just about any type of paper)
Paper towels
Plastic comb with sturdy teeth (optional)
Clothespins, preferably plastic
Drying rack
Appropriate paint thinner for cleaning up

To make marbleized paper:
1. Cover a large, clean, dry surface (a large table, or even the floor) with plenty of newspaper. Change the newspaper as often as necessary. There should be enough flat space on this work surface to allow you to put a completed sheet of painted paper on it to dry, after you remove it from the

water. By placing it on the newspaper, you also help remove excess water from the paper as well.

2. Fill the tray with a few inches of lukewarm water.
3. Following the directions on the can, spray the primary color in the water. Spray other colors in the water and note how they seem to "float" on it.
4. Run a sheet of the watercolor paper across the tray of water, catching the paint on it. Some paint will not adhere. If too much adheres, blot the paper *very carefully* with paper towels, so as not to ruin the marbleized effect. If a good deal of paint has adhered, run a plastic comb through different areas of the paper to make parallel striations of color. Then, if necessary, blot carefully.
5. Using a clothespin, carefully hang the paper from one corner on a drying rack. Allow it to dry completely before using.

Newsprint

Newsprint may be less exotic, but it is infinitely less costly than most of the papers previously described. Newsprint needn't be a boring gift wrap, either. Remember, newspapers are printed in just about every language. Imagine how interesting a medley of Arabic, Russian, Greek, English, and Italian would look! The perfect gift wrap paper for a going-away present would be newspaper from the country that the lucky recipient is going to visit. A collection of foreign-language newspapers would make an excellent collage.

Even if you are confined to using only your local paper(s), there is still no reason that newspaper gift wrap has to look uncreative. Notice the variations in the print of different papers and different sections of them.

Use a particular paper or section of the paper to reflect the occasion—the sports page for a person who made the tennis team; the apartment listings for a housewarming present, and so on.

For a child's present, save the Sunday comics. Add a big multicolored bow with a small Snoopy or Paddington Bear in the middle, or try a few small balloons tied to a large bow—what could be more festive!

Newsprint has another advantage: you can cut out large letters from headlines to spell something across the top of the box—the recipient's name, or a message like "Bon Voyage." Circle the letters around the box, making the recipient guess the secret word, which could be a clue as to what is inside the box.

Kraft Paper

This is heavy brown wrapping paper that is usually reserved for mailing packages; it needn't be. Kraft paper, like newspaper, can be embellished in a variety of ways (see Vegetable Printing in the section on Tissue Paper). Apply gleaming cut-out stars in a geometric pattern, or strew them randomly across the top of a box.

A bunch of dried flowers can look handsome and is also inexpensive. Try a bunch of eucalyptus leaves on kraft paper, or dried statice (pick lavender and gold for contrast). Make leaves from construction, tissue, or crepe paper. Pick a coordinated-color ribbon to make a big three-dimensional bow, holding the "bouquet" together.

Maps

Old maps and new maps—even run-of-the-mill roadmaps found in the glove compartment—can make colorful wrapping paper. (*See Color Plate 14.*) Make notations on the map that would have significance to the recipient. Or make a "trail" on the map—to the easiest way to open the box, to the card, to special instructions, to a place on the map that the recipient is going to visit, etc.

For the boating enthusiast, set a toy sailboat asea on a body of water. Hoist your gift card or tag on the sail.

For a birthday present, a moving-away present, or a retirement gift, you might use a map of the state where he/she grew up and mark points of interest from "life's highway" with map pins. Maps will provide you with a great deal of inspiration.

Computer Print-out Paper

This kind of paper is great because it comes in large quantities and emerges from the computer neatly accordion-folded. Computer print-out paper is admittedly not very glamorous, but it could come in handy to easily wrap around a large gift like a huge box containing a new stove. For a special touch you might wish to decorate this paper with cut-outs from magazines, or stickers.

Sheet Music

Sheet music can provide many interesting possibilities for gift wrapping. (*See Color Plate 6.*) It's an ideal wrap for a gift to a friend who is aspiring to be a piano virtuoso or an opera star, for example. Photocopy a particular aria or keyboard passage onto a slightly lighter-weight paper, which may be easier for wrapping purposes. Sheet music might be the perfect gift wrap for a pair of tickets to a concert or other musical performance.

Posters

Posters are an endless source for large-sized wrapping papers. Check with local travel agencies about taking a few travel posters home. Select those that are of the lightest-weight stock so that you can fold them. Use heavyweight posters to plaster on the sides of large boxes. Other sources of oversized, dramatic, or unusual posters are movie theaters, concert halls, civic centers, or community cultural centers.

Shelf-lining Paper

This paper is available in discount or variety stores, is very lightweight, and is easy to fold. Some shelf-lining papers are very sheer plastic, so be careful, as they tear easily.

These papers are available in long rolls and are usually only about 18 inches wide. Many have coordinated trimmings (usually pleated, scalloped, or quilted) that are meant to run along shelf edges but could easily be put to use on a wrapped package.

Self-adhesive Papers

Self-adhesive papers may be purchased in discount and hardware stores, as well as art supply stores. (Ask what they have in addition to fancy mylar films.) These papers, generally used for covering shelves and counter tops, are also very attractive as gift wraps. (*See Tie Package in Color Plate 1.*) Adhesive-backed papers, such as silver mylar and other high-gloss colors, are fun to work with because they don't require glue and can be cut into shapes, peeled, and instantly adhered. They also serve as good coverings for boxes that might be used for other purposes in the future—such as a hatbox that could be used for storage after the gift has been removed.

Adhesive-backed papers are usually available by the yard, and are generally not very wide—18 inches at most. They are available in a great variety of patterns and solid colors, often with several prints coordinated in a single color scheme.

One particularly useful paper on the market comes in several different textures, including a velvetlike surface and a burlap weave. The sheets are approximately 12 × 10 inches. This paper is ideal to decorate the top of a package that is wrapped in a solid-colored or small printed paper. For example, if you want to put a bouquet of flowers on plain kraft paper, use a burlaplike self-adhesive paper in shades of natural, gold, brown, and beige to form different petal shapes, which make a small floral offering. Simply by peeling the backing away, you can adhere the "petals" to the kraft paper. An instant bouquet! Or, work small geometric pieces into a random design. (*See Color Plate 2.*)

Wallpaper

This is another nontraditional wrapping paper. Get an out-of-date wallpaper book from your local shop or distributor. The sample pieces are small, but ideal for wrapping tiny presents, Christmas stocking-stuffers, or jewelry. The small swatches that have designs or prints lend themselves to being cut up. For example, a pattern with teddy bears may provide you with six bears you can paste on a package for a small child, or a pattern with a crazy-quilt design may work well on a gift for someone who sews.

Construction Paper

Construction paper may be found in discount, stationery, and party-goods stores, as well as in art supply stores. You are more likely to find a suitable, lightweight paper at the first three. The cheaper the paper, the more likely it is to be thin enough for gift wrapping. Even if the paper is too heavy for wrapping a package, you can still use it for embellishing gifts.

Construction paper is available in a variety of sizes, from the standard 8½ × 11-inch, or 10 × 11-inch dimensions to large 24 × 36-inch sheets.

Although standard construction paper comes in rather dull colors, don't dismiss it just for that reason. It is very suitable for use by small children, particularly for making coordinated cards for presents.

Seamless Paper

This is paper used by photographers as a backdrop for their photo sessions (so that they get a solid-colored background); it is also terrific for use in gift wrapping. Seamless paper comes in a soft palette of colors—even the most vibrant red is somewhat subdued. This is a stiff paper, meant to withstand heavy use, but it is also an ideal paper for making ornaments and adornments for packages. Seamless paper will work better for making sophisticated decorations than will standard construction paper because of its weight, and, of course, it has the advantage of size. If you have a friend in the photography business, ask him or her to save you some seamless paper before it is discarded, since it is unlikely that you'd buy a whole roll yourself.

Foil Papers

Foil papers are especially good for wrapping packages with unusual shapes. They are quite pliant and can be molded to almost any form—just as you mold aluminum foil over a bowl for storage in the refrigerator. (And don't dismiss that product, either; you can use it in an emergency.) Foils come in a multitude of very bright colors, often with a reverse of another color or a "plain" silver. One type of foil will tear; other new, more resilient foils—called polyfoils—will not tear. You will find solids, stripes, and embossed prints among the offerings.

FABRICS

While gift wrapping papers will probably grace most of the packages you wrap, don't overlook fabrics for a change of pace. Fabrics are much more versatile and flexible than most papers, and sometimes using a fabric will allow you to employ small, otherwise useless, remnants you have around your home. Here are some of the many uses for fabric in gift wrapping:

• wrap the entire box, as you would with paper

• wrap the lid and bottom half of the box separately, so that you create a box that can be used in the future, for storage of treasured personal items

• envelop the gift in fabric, *inside* the box, as an interesting alternative to tissue paper

• cut strips of fabric from long remnants, with a pinking shears, and use the strips as ribbons and ties

• decorate a wrapped present with cut-outs and adornments made of fabric

• fabric can be easily wrapped around odd-shaped gifts, such as a football; just wrap the fabric around and tie both ends to make a firecracker finish (see Chapter Three, "Wrapping a Cylinder or Drum")

• make novelty wrapping that you could not make with paper, employing such items as lace ruffles or denim (see descrip-

tion of "Welcome to New York City" present, mentioned later in
this chapter)

• use tiny scraps of fabric to cover a box lid and the bottom half
of the box; glue on the pieces individually in a pastiche to resemble a crazy quilt. (*See Color Plate 15.*)

To Make a Patchwork Crazy-quilt Box

Materials:
Box to be covered
Newspaper
Assortment of remnants and scraps of fabric, coordinated or
    varied in color; shapes can be circular, irregular, geometric, or
    as desired
Pinking shears
Spray adhesive, suitable for fabrics
Trimming scissors

(*Note:* As in all projects, have a large, flat work area available,
free from dirt and unnecessary objects. This type of wrapping
works best with a box that has a separate lid, designed with a
shallow lip, so that the lid "sits" on top of the bottom half of
the box and leaves most of that bottom half exposed. This way,
all your handiwork can be seen and enjoyed.)

To cover the box:
1. Keep the work surface covered with plenty of fresh, clean
   newspaper; replenish it as you work, so that the fabrics stay
   clean.
2. Cut up fabric scraps with pinking shears to keep the cut
   edges from fraying. Set the fabric pieces aside, out of the
   reach of the spray adhesive.
3. Take about six scraps, turn them wrong side up on the newspaper, and spray a fine film of glue over them. Randomly
   adhere them to the lid of the box, starting from one corner
   or edge and working toward the other side of the lid. Press
   them in place.

4. Take another six or eight scraps and proceed the same way. As you spray, be certain that the box is out of the way of the spray. Continue adding patchwork pieces until the entire lid is covered. Trim around the lip of the lid.
5. Cover the bottom of the box in the same fashion.
6. If desired, the interior of both the box and the lid may be covered in this manner, making this box a present in itself, one that the recipient can use for storage as well as decorative purposes.

Just about any fabric is suitable for wrapping purposes. Here are some hints:

COTTONS AND LIGHTWEIGHT SHEERS are ideal for wrapping a gift as you would with paper, since they are light enough to make corners and be tucked under; use a very lightweight sheer fabric, such as organdy, with another color fabric underneath it for a special present for a wedding, shower, engagement, baby gift, etc.

POPLINS AND HEAVIER-WEIGHT COTTONS are good for wrapping regular boxes and problem shapes, such as a bottle of wine or a bulky sweater that didn't come with a gift box.

CHINTZ, a brightly printed fabric that was once considered a workhorse fabric for upholstery and housecoats, can be quite expensive; these remnants can be used on almost any type of gift, and the glazed finish of the fabric will enhance the wrapping nicely.

CANVAS OR DUCK (a strong, tightly woven fabric) are lightweight enough to wrap around oddly shaped gifts that require more support than a cotton wrapping—such as a tennis racket or an umbrella.

DENIM, BURLAP, and other less malleable heavyweight fabrics can be used for novelty purposes, such as appliqués or decorations. (*See Color Plate 1, denim pocket.*)

BROCADE, FLOCKED CLOTH, UPHOLSTERY FABRIC, AND VELVETS bring a feeling of luxe with them, and should, therefore, be confined to gifts that also have that aura; in other words, don't wrap a basketball in flocked velvet. Use a dressy fabric to line the inside of a lacquered basket that is filled with expensive bath, boudoir, or cosmetic items; or use flocked velvet to surround a piece of crystal *inside* a box.

FELT—technically, *not* a fabric, since it is not woven, but rather matted or "felted" together—will provide endless inspiration for use by both adults and children. Felt will never unravel; it's inexpensive; and there are a lot of lovely colors from which to choose. Make package decorations with felt, or use large sheets of it to cover oversized gifts such as a bicycle. Felt may be used to wrap up awkward shapes that need support, like an easel or a pair of skis.

What are some novel ways to use fabric? I once used a pocket from a pair of denim jeans for a gift that can only be described as a "Welcome to New York City" present. The gift was for a good friend who was moving here from the country. Another friend and I bought city, bus, and subway maps; a book that showed the seating plans of major Broadway theaters; over a dozen subway tokens; a guide book of walking tours; a restaurant review book; and other items we thought would make her move easier. We wrapped all the gifts individually in various New York newspapers and tied each with a very bright ribbon. Everything was placed in a large box that we wrapped in yellow paper.

Using craft glue suitable for fabrics, I adhered a denim pocket, cut from an old pair of jeans, to the center of the wrapped package. Inside the pocket, I tucked a red country-style bandanna. The country-style wrapping was perfect for the occasion, and our friend was delighted.

You might use the same idea—the denim-jeans pocket (*see Color Plate 1*)—for any number of occasions:

• a trip to visit friends in the country, a house gift for friends out-of-town

• a gift for heralding spring, or a gift for a gardener friend

• a novelty present for a child

Inside the kerchief or bandanna, you could put any number of surprises or treats:

• some jelly beans

• a tiny paint set for your *artiste* friend, who will probably want to use the bandanna as well

• a miniature game for a child

• an initial key chain or a monogram pin

• a key to a new car

• a gift certificate

OTHER PACKAGE COVERINGS AND EMBELLISHMENTS

Great gift wrapping materials can be found around the home, in the garage, in the attic, in the basement, and anywhere else you may have squirreled away things you never use.

Plastic Storage Bags

These bags can be used as special, nontraditional containers for your wrapping needs. The dark green color of lawn bags, for instance, will keep the recipient of a present from knowing what is inside. To further conceal a gift, you can pad its shape with lots of newspaper, tissue paper, or rings of corrugated cardboard. Tie a large bow around the top, and perhaps staple a few smaller bows around the bag, randomly spaced.

White kitchen bags can be decorated with stickers, decals, seals, or grease pencil or waterproof marker graffiti. For example, for Valentine's Day, an oversized gift might be put in a white kitchen bag filled with red tissue paper, decorated on the outside with little red stick-on hearts, and tied with a big red ribbon. (*See Color Plate 17.*)

A clear bag might be decorated from the inside out, by filling it with wads of crushed-up, gaily colored tissue paper, thereby concealing the gift under the decorative spray of color.

Ties for the necks of these bags may be thick yarn, rope, large strips of fabric, or even boat line.

Sheets, Blankets, Cloths

Sheets can be dyed a bold, dramatic color to make them more festive for use in gift wrapping. You might also apply the dye with a paint brush, since hand-painted fabrics can look quite stylish. Dilute the dye and paint. If you're not Picasso, so what? The gift will be wrapped with lots of personal feeling. Try spray paint for an overall misty effect.

If you have an old blanket that is in good shape, you can use it to wrap a new pair of skis.

An old shower curtain, either plastic or fabric, can be great to use in gift wrapping when it has a lovely print or design on it. Old curtains can provide cushioning or padding for a gift.

Sheets of plastic, or clear plastic on a roll might work well for an oversized gift. Clear plastic can be transformed with dye, to get a warm, transparent glow of a particular tone. A colorful painters' dropcloth or a movers' pad—not too worn or soiled—might also work nicely to enclose a large housewarming gift.

You will probably amaze yourself with your own inventiveness once you start trying different possibilities for wraps.

Doilies

While paper doilies are not necessarily good for wrapping whole packages, they are still very versatile. (*See Color Plate 17.*) Cut them up to make decorations on the outside of packages, or wrap a tiny bouquet of violets in a doily, or present a linen handkerchief in one. They may be used to make appliqués on a wrapped gift, or as a stencil (see instructions below).

You will find doilies in white, gold and silver, red, green, pink, yellow, and blue. Holidays reveal a new panoply of colors: with Halloween and Thanksgiving come brown, orange, beige, and deep gold doilies; Easter brings out all the pastel shades; for Valentine's Day there are red heart-shaped doilies, often in metallic finishes; for St. Patrick's Day, metallic green shamrocks; in June, silver wedding bells.

Doilies come in different shapes—circles, squares, rectangles, triangles. There are also many kinds of novelty doilies in party stores, especially at holiday time. (*See illustration in Chapter Six, in the section about Doilies.*)

To Use a Doily as a Stencil

Materials:
1 doily, selected size and shape
Double-stick tape
Newspaper
Spray paint, color-coordinated with the gift wrap paper

How to do it:
1. Place the doily on the package, where desired (centered will generally look best). Pick a part of the doily where there is no cut work and use a few tiny pieces of double-stick tape to secure the doily to the package.
2. Surround the wrapped package with plenty of newspaper and mask the sides of the box, as well.
3. Gently spray the package with the paint, using a light mist. Two coats of a lightly sprayed film are better than one heavy coat. Allow to dry.
4. When the paint is dry, gently remove the doily.

Here are some other ideas for using doilies to decorate packages or presents:

• Cut a large square or round doily into quarters. Glue each quarter to a corner of the box. Glue a small bow at each corner, to embellish the doilies.

• Cut a large circular doily into pie slices, each one eighth of the circle. Glue them to the package, leaving a 1-inch space between each slice of the pie. Attach a bow in the center.

• Cut several small round doilies in half. Select doilies that are no more than 3 to 4 inches in diameter. Place them, cut edge to cut edge, along an imaginary center line, but not directly aligned so that they form the circles you just cut in half. Place them so that they are 2 inches off-center, forming wavy scallops.

• Cut triangular-shaped pieces from the corners of a square or rectangular doily. Place the triangles in a line, along an imaginary center line on the package, all with the original corner of the doily pointing in the same direction. The doilies can overlap or touch, depending on the size of the package.

Plastic Films

These are another staple item in party-goods stores. They differ from those in art supply stores by being more economical, flexible enough for gift wrapping, and available in a small selection of colors. (Art supply stores stock a greater supply of colors because that is where artists go for their professional needs.)

Plastic films in party stores are usually called Polythane™, a moisture-proof, heat-sealable wrapping. It is quite malleable and ideal for wrapping odd-shaped boxes, baskets of fruit, homemade candies, biscuits and other goodies, as well as cumbersome presents. (*See Candle Package in Color Plate 5.*) However, be aware that most plastic films should not be used in direct contact with food; there is a warning to that effect on some packages.

Cardboards

Lightweight cardboards and show-card boards are usually available in party-goods stores in a great panoply of colors, even metallics. These materials are much too heavy to use for gift wrapping a package. However, they are good, inexpensive sources of large, pretty papers for covering big surfaces, or for wrapping around odd shapes, such as tennis rackets.

Corrugated cardboards are a little too heavy for gift wrapping, but they are well suited to use for hard-to-wrap objects with odd shapes and no box, such as a globe. At the party-goods store, you will find large sheets of beautifully colored cardboard that is corrugated on one side only, so that it is very flexible. This is one of my favorite materials for wrapping large, unwieldy objects.

RIBBONS

At the beginning of this chapter, we mentioned different types of materials that can be used as substitutes for traditional ribbons. A yarn store is an excellent warehouse for the many possibilities. Don't be put off by ropes and twines with unfamiliar textures; and don't overlook that clothesline in the hardware store or the cotton mop replacements. Those hanks of limp mop fibers can be cut up, dyed, or used as they are—they would make a great lion's mane or hairdo for a funny face on top of a package for a child. (*See Color Plate 6.*) Triple-ply yarns can be coiled on the top of a package to make a colorful design. But before you get too involved with experimentation, learn fully what is on the market for you to use.

Standard Gift Wrapping Ribbons

This is probably the most abundant type of ribbon in your house. The most popular kinds include:

• narrow, ribbed ribbon that curls when a scissor blade is run over it

• high-gloss, rayon-based ribbon that has a satiny sheen to it on both sides; this ribbon sticks to itself when moistened

• inexpensive cloth ribbons with cut-and-fused edges; they are inexpensively priced and are most common in the florist industry

• paper ribbons that come in a variety of prints and designs; they will add great drama to a package and are nominal in price

Woven Cloth Ribbons

These ribbons are meant for home sewing, decorating, and more expensive applications than gift wrapping; but for extra-special presents, you may very well want to splurge on them. They are found in the notions, sewing, and decorating departments of large stores, not in the stationery department; nor are you likely to find good-quality cloth ribbons with woven edges in a party-goods store. Unlike ribbons used by florists, their designs are woven into them, not printed on.

Woven cloth ribbons come in about as many varieties as does cloth: velvet, taffeta, moiré, silk, satin, grosgrain, cotton, etc. Many cloth ribbons are even two-sided. Some have fancy scalloping, called *picot,* along their edges.

Homemade "Ribbon"

One way to make printed, decorated, patterned ribbon is to use cloth that you have in the scrap bin. Use a pinking shears and cut long, thin strips of fabric—you'll have instant ribbon. If you cut on the bias, your "ribbon" will also have stretch to it, thus lengthening its mileage.

If you have odd-shaped pieces of fabric from your sewing, you can pink the strips unevenly, so that the ribbon edges snake in thick and thin curves.

No matter what type of ribbon you use, always save the scraps. You can put them to use in any number of ways:

• Tie the handles of a shopping bag together with a tiny scrap; be sure to coordinate the color with the color of the bag, the tissue paper inside the bag, or the gift itself.

• Scraps of ribbon of the same color family can make a lovely flower for the top of a package. After the box is wrapped and a ribbon has been tied around it, lay the small (5 inches or so) scraps across the knot of the package's ribbon, placing them diagonally across the knot in several directions. Tie the final knot of the bow and all the short ends of ribbon will flare out like a flower. Cut the ends of ribbon on a slant and you will have a flower bow.

• Use mix-and-match small bits of ribbon to write the recipient's name on the top of the package, in bold, block letters; use double-stick tape to hold the ribbon in place.

BOXES

You would think that this would be the easy part of wrapping a present—what is there to a box? Actually, a lot. Not that you have to study this topic as an engineer would. What you must learn is to pick the appropriate type of box for the gift you are giving.

Not all stores give you a box when you make a purchase, and some items almost never come in a box (like a basketball or a baseball bat). In lieu of buying a box at a discount store or party-goods shop, you may have to scout around the house for one that will do, or else simply make one. If you are hunting for a box, be aware of the various factors that will affect your choice—style, color, strength, size, and shape.

Rigid Boxes

Rigid boxes are the best containers for most gifts because they are firm and always come with a detachable lid. The lid of the box will have a lip to it, which may extend a bit over the side of the bottom half of the box, or all the way to the bottom of it.

Collapsible Boxes

These boxes vary in durability, ranging from good quality to flimsy. In the latter case, you might be better off with no box at all. Consider the collapsible box that a loaf-style cake comes in from the bakery; it is fine, and quite appropriate for the cake, but wouldn't be at all suitable to contain a heavy pair of roller skates.

If you shop for boxes around the time of special holidays, you may find some pretty and unusual specimens.

• At Christmastime there are novelty boxes for children's gifts that look like milk cartons. Such boxes may be printed to resemble a house, and may even have Santa Claus climbing across the roof into the chimney.

• Valentine's Day always brings heart-shaped candy boxes, which you should save. A heart-shaped box can be covered with sheer lace fabric for a gift of feminine lace handkerchiefs. The box also can become a permanent place to store other treasured items.

• Easter brings many egg-shaped containers as well as a variety of pretty, gaily colored baskets. Save some Easter basket supplies —especially the artificial "grass," which makes good padding for other gifts.

CUTTING TOOLS

The most important cutting implement you will use is, of course, a pair of scissors. You should have a pair of paper shears for your gift wrapping tasks and confine the use of those shears to paper only. If you use different kinds of scissors (see below) for their intended purposes, you will keep each pair in optimum condition longer.

The following cutting tools will be useful to you for your gift wrapping needs:

PAPER SHEARS have long, slender blades and usually measure a minimum of 8 inches from the tip of the blades to the end of the circular holes that act as the handles. Both blades meet in a point that allows you to cut around fine areas. The blades should make long, clean cuts. If they stick, "grab" the paper, or lose their "bite," it is time to have them reconditioned and sharpened.

DRESSMAKERS' SHEARS should be used for cutting fabrics. One blade is usually pointed and the other curved, allowing for diverse fabric applications.

PINKING SHEARS should be used when you are working with fabrics that you don't want to unravel, or for making ribbons from fabrics. You can also cut paper with pinking shears, for a decorative edge.

EMBROIDERY SCISSORS, SMALL TRIMMERS, OR SILHOUETTE SCISSORS may be necessary if you are doing any very small, delicate, detailed work.

MAT KNIFE: This can be used to cut heavier papers, cardboards, or mat boards. Don't attempt to cut heavyweight papers with paper shears—you'll ruin them. Be certain to purchase a mat knife with a retractable blade.

UTILITY KNIFE: This is a small but invaluable tool; it is similar to a mat knife but is very tiny. It has a small blade attached to a penlike shank, making it ideal to clip edges or get into hard-to-reach spots (on cut-outs, for example), and slice through cardboard to score it. Buy an X-acto knife that comes with a cover for the blade.

TAPES

Tapes come in different widths—the most common for gift wrapping are ½ inch and 1 inch. Wider tapes are available, but unless you are using strapping tape or sealing tape to mail a package you will almost never need tape wider than 1 inch.

CELLOPHANE TAPE is the most common type of tape, and it comes in two basic varieties: a crystal-clear product (the original); and a newer, somewhat translucent tape, called Magic Tape by its manufacturer, the 3M Company. Magic Tape becomes invisible once it is pressed down, and it can also be written on.

DOUBLE-STICK TAPE will adhere to whatever surface you put it on; likewise, whatever you put onto the tape will adhere to *it*. Here are a few decorating ideas:

• Form parallel stripes of double-stick tape on top of a package and sprinkle glitter over them; or apply rickrack or some other trimming to them.

• "Draw" circles of tape; place miniature pompons over the tape, then place one pompon in the center, and you've made "flowers."

• Spell out a message with tape and then sprinkle rice or crushed corn flakes over it.

DECORATIVE TAPES include all sorts of different-colored plastic tapes sold in hardware stores, notions departments, and stationery stores. Use them to decorate and embellish a package, to write a message on the box, or to make designs on the outside of the package.

MASKING TAPE is very useful around the home, but not very practical for gift wrapping. Nevertheless, you might still wish to try these decorating ideas:

• "Dye" it with colored marker or shoe polish.

• Cut shapes to form a design, something that might look good on brown kraft paper.

GLUES

GLUE STICKS are tubes of tacky glue, in solid form, packaged like lipsticks. They are:

• easy to work with, for both fabric and paper

• ideal for small touch-up jobs

• good for repositioning work

• simple to clean up—from your hands, as well as the package (if you've put too much glue on the wrong place)

• inexpensive

RUBBER CEMENT is a dependable product that is:

• well suited for use with paper

• very easy to clean up from your hands and from the package

• inexpensive

• an easy product to store, and it keeps a long time if the jar is well sealed

WHITE GLUES are just that—white, creamy glues, that usually come in large, squeeze-style containers. They are:

• water-soluble for easy cleanup (with a damp cotton swab)

• easy to apply—squeeze some on the spot, or use a paint brush for easy coverage of a large area

• perfect for craft items; use it for sequins, baubles, fabric trims, plastics, foils, glitter, and paper

• easy to work with; they set quickly, dry crystal clear (like a hard plastic), and are nontoxic

Spray adhesives come in aerosol cans and produce a fine mist of glue. They are perfect for applying to large surface areas, but the adhesive is not very strong. Spray adhesives are multipurpose and are good to have on hand because they:

• allow for repositioning (the sprayed paper or fabric) without making a mess

• are adaptable to both fabric and paper

• are economical; a little goes a long way (a small amount creates a fine mist over a large surface area)

• do not bleed through the material that is sprayed

(*Note:* To keep the nozzle clog-free, always hold the can upside down and spray until the spraying mechanism empties itself; then clean it. Lightly moisten a cotton ball with nail polish remover, and wipe it over the nozzle. Then pierce the spray hole with a pin.)

These are the supplies and equipment that I think will be the most useful to you for gift wrapping. But this does not mean that they are the only products you will use. After you have the opportunity to work with diverse products, you will develop your own favorites.

A word of caution: A very popular glue that has recently proliferated in the market is "instant glue." This glue bonds, as it advertises, instantly. It also bonds *skin* instantly, which is a purpose for which it was once used quite regularly—in certain surgical procedures for the bonding of tissues.

Originally these glues were available only for nonporous surfaces, but now a second generation of instant glues has been developed, for porous surfaces. If, for some reason, you wish to use an "instant" or "super glue," use it precisely as directed, and *never* allow a child to use the product.

CHAPTER
THREE

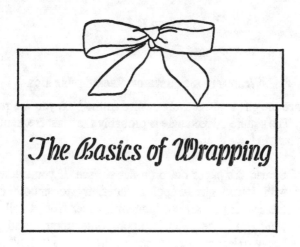

The Basics of Wrapping

$\mathcal{S}$ince you have probably wrapped dozens, if not hundreds, of packages prior to reading this book, you most likely already know a good deal about this subject. The tricks discussed in this chapter will utilize fairly standard techniques, but show you how to wrap more professionally and how to handle unusual wrapping challenges.

BOX SELECTION

First of all, here are some guidelines to select the best box or package for your present:

• Select a box that is appropriate to the gift in style and texture. A beautiful piece of china would look nice in a pretty silver box.

• Pick the correct size box, based on the height and width of your gift. The present shouldn't look crammed or "lost at sea" in the box.

• Choose a box with the proper strength for the gift's weight. Be particularly careful if the present is a heavy, breakable one—allow extra room around it for padding.

Wrapping a Square or Rectangular Box

Once the gift is attractively nestled in the box, you are ready to wrap. The square or rectangle is probably the most frequent shape that you will have to cover.

1. Spread the paper out on a flat surface. If you are working with folded gift wrapping paper, try to smooth out the creases. If you are working with paper from a roll, unroll what you judge to be the appropriate amount, and place a heavy object at each corner, so that the ends don't roll up.
2. Place the box near one edge of the paper, leaving about a 2-inch margin.
3. Flip the box over three times, which will give you a fairly accurate measure of the amount of paper you'll need in one direction. Add another 2 inches to that measurement and mark the spot with a light pencil mark or a snip at the edge of the paper.
4. Return the box to the edge of the paper as in Step #2. Stand the box up on its other side and flip it over twice, so that it ends up standing on the opposite side. That is where you will cut the paper in that direction.
5. Return the box to the mark that you made in Step #3. Cut the paper in the other direction. Now you are ready to wrap the box.
6. Place the box in the center of the cut piece of paper, the top side down.
7. Mark an imaginary straight line across the center of the bottom of the box; bring up one edge of the cut paper to that straight line and pull it about 1 inch beyond (*Fig. 1*). Be sure that the paper makes a straight line. Use a few small pieces of tape to secure the paper to the box.

COLOR PLATE 1

Three simple packages made with appliqués. The Tie, Mitten, and Denim Pocket Packages are all described in detail in Chapter Seven.

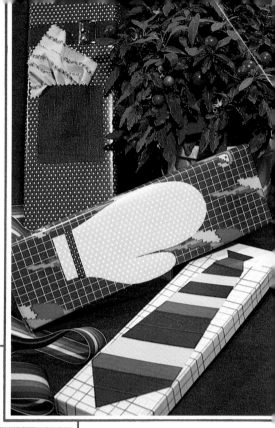

COLOR PLATE 2

Two types of wrappings suitable for a man. One is ideal for a shirt; the other is suitable for anything from a lawn hose to desk accessories. Both are described in Chapter Seven.

COLOR PLATE 3

(Above) Here is a great Christmas wrapping idea employing a novelty sled that was saved from a previous Christmas. After the present is opened, the sled and its contents can be used as a tabletop decoration or ornamentation for the mantel. Also note that the two packages on the left are wrapped with scraps of ribbon, as described in the Zinnia flower instructions. (Christmas wreath designed by Gwen Evrard).

COLOR PLATE 4

This wrapping — ideal on a gift for a newborn or soon-to-be born child — makes use of a novelty bassinet and a handful of "balloons" that are made over Styrofoam balls. The jelly beans are an added treat. This package could contain anything from a complete dinner set to clothing.

(Above) Birthday cheer in two delightful packages described in Chapter Seven: Candlelight and Colored Crayons.

Mr. Mop Top, two record albums, and the Piano Package — all featuring a black-and-white motif, each containing different gifts. Mr. Mop Top houses a bottle of spirits; the Piano Package could hold some type of apparel, a book, or a home accessory.

COLOR PLATE 7

Several ways to wrap a bottle of alcohol (from left to right): a land-
scape, with a glass phial attached to the package, holding a fresh
flower; a Cherry Tomato/Strawberry Package, described in Chapter
Seven; a chimney made with a self-adhesive decorative paper, with
a miniature Santa Claus (a honeycomb ornament) perched on top;
the Magical Space Ship, described in Chapter Seven; and the cloth
sack, which can easily be made with just a small piece of material.

A variety of methods for wrapping small jewelry boxes. The Zinnia flower is described in Chapter Six, and the Jeweled Mushroom is described in Chapter Seven.

A detail of the Zinnia flower.

COLOR PLATE 10

See Chapter Seven for instructions to make this charming bird. It is even more delightful to look at here, balanced in a basketful of eggs.

The Umbrella Package and the
Sumptuous Ribbon Roses box —
two enticing treatments for tall,
oversized boxes.

COLOR PLATE 12

A detail of the ribbon roses.
Notice how lifelike they are.

COLOR PLATE 13

A splendid Zinnia flower is on the right, made entirely from scraps saved from other wrappings. On the left is a simple package, the focal point of which is a large honeycomb decoration.

8. Bring up the other edge of the paper, overlapping it over the tape. Turn under the excess paper, making a hem (*Fig. 2*). Be sure that your fold is straight. Neatness is essential.
9. Tape the hemmed edge in place, running the tape parallel to the edge of the paper, *not* perpendicular to it. (If you wish to be particularly neat, use double-stick tape on the turned-under part of hem so that no tape shows at all on the outside of your package.)
10. To make "hospital bed" corners—for a neat, crisp look to the wrapping—fold down the excess paper along the open edge on one side of the box, pushing the paper well into each corner. If this flap of paper is too long for the side of the box, trim away the excess (*Fig. 3*). Crease the two sides (*Fig. 4*).
11. Fold the two creased flaps inward, toward the middle (*Fig. 5*), and crease them against the box (*Fig. 6*). Tape them together if they overlap, or tape them to the paper flap, made in Step #10, if they don't overlap.
12. Bring up the flap that you have just created, so that it covers the side and comes up over the bottom of the box.
13. Crease this flap along both the top and bottom edges of the box, folding the excess paper under, making a hem that will be flush with the edge of the box.
14. Secure this flap in place with tape, running it parallel to the hem (*Fig. 7*). (You could use double-stick tape, as suggested in Step #9.)
15. Repeat Steps #10–14 on the other open end.

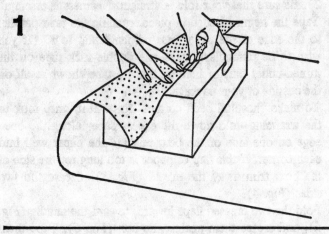

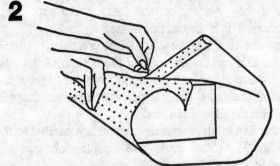

3

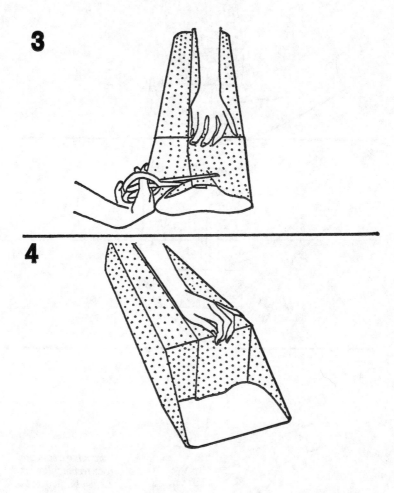

4

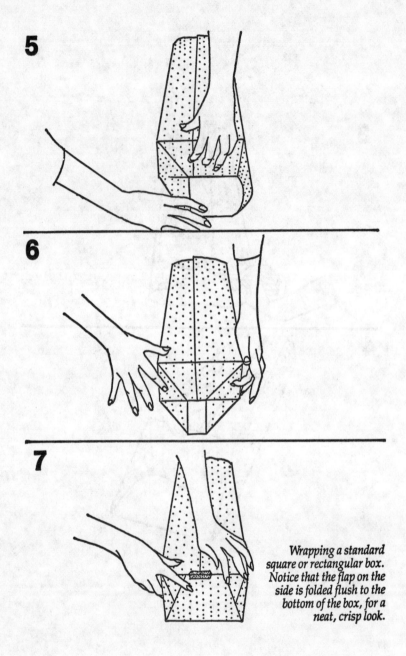

5

6

7

Wrapping a standard square or rectangular box. Notice that the flap on the side is folded flush to the bottom of the box, for a neat, crisp look.

Wrapping a Cylinder or Drum

There are two simple ways to wrap a cylinder—whether it's a short, squat box of dusting powder, a child's toy drum, or a long, skinny tube containing a poster.

This variety of cylinder-shaped packages, wrapped with diverse finishes — fanciful and tailored — are all easy to make.

1. Determine the amount of paper that you will need to cover the container by rolling the wrapping paper around the circumference of the box. Allow for two extra inches, cut the paper, and secure it with tape.
2. Allow for enough paper to cover the ends of the cylinder or drum. You will always need at least as much paper on each end as the measurement of one half the diameter of the container.

3. There are several ways to finish the ends of a wrapped cylinder. The method you choose will be determined largely by the size of the end of the container. In general, a container with a small diameter will look neater with firecracker ends; one with a large diameter will look better with pleated ends.

Firecracker Finishes:

• After the paper has been secured around the cylinder, gather in the ends, bunching up the paper. Fasten securely with a ribbon.

• Once the ends are secured, you can fringe the paper, cutting it into small, spaghettilike strips, or you can leave it gathered and somewhat fluted.

• If you roll several layers of different colors of tissue paper around the cylinder before putting the gift wrapping paper around it, then you will have many more layers of paper to gather in at the ends, which makes the cylinder look very festive.

Pleated Finishes:

• After the paper is rolled around the cylinder and taped in place (*Fig. 1*), press the excess paper down to the surface of the cylinder at one end, using your finger to push a section of paper about 1 inch wide. Press the paper down against the edge of the container and create a crease (*Fig. 2*). When you have the bit of paper folded down, move your finger to the side and press down again, forcing another inch of paper down to the surface of the cylinder's end (*Fig. 3*).

• Continue to move your finger around the edge of the cylinder, pressing the excess paper down over it, forcing it into small pleats. Press down at even intervals, so that the pleats are about the same size.

• When you reach the point where you started, try to force that last pleat under the first one, so that the pleating appears continuous (*Fig. 4*).

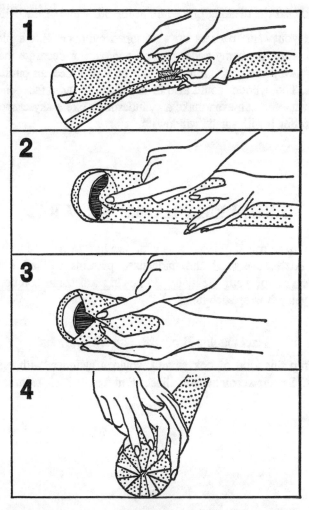

Wrapping a standard cylinder shape with a "pleated" finish. Don't force too much paper down when making the pleats; it's better to have many small, crisp pleats than many large, sloppy pleats.

• Secure with a small piece of tape.

• Repeat the pleating procedure at the other end of the cylinder.

• If you want to dress up a wrapped cylinder with a pleated finish, you can simply add a bow on one end; or decorate the cylinder as a person, with a mop of hair on top, a face, an outfit, and shoes. The cylinder could also be made into a large face—such as a clown. You can even make a cylinder look like a skyscraper, by decorating it with small "windows."

PROBLEM SHAPES TO WRAP

Unboxed round objects; gifts with peculiar forms; strangely faceted boxes; oversized and undersized presents will all provide challenges for your creativity. Following are some solutions to help you gift wrap such items.

Rectangular Box with Curved Corners

Wrap this kind of box as you would a cylinder, with pleated ends. (See the accompanying illustration for the basic technique to use.)

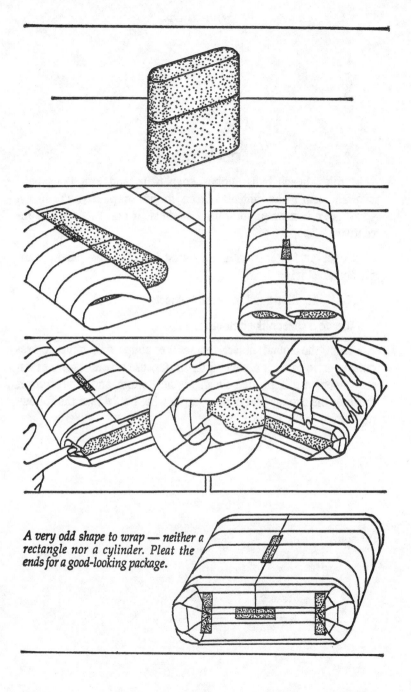

A very odd shape to wrap — neither a rectangle nor a cylinder. Pleat the ends for a good-looking package.

Round Objects

Marbles, beach balls, globes, soap balls, and Ping-Pong balls may all seem to be difficult objects to gift wrap. If you're lucky, you'll get a box when you purchase them. If not, you must be inventive.

• Cover such items with narrow strips of crepe paper, completely enveloping them.

• Roll yarn all around the round object.

• Create a gazebolike holder for it.

• Treat the round object like a box shape and wrap it firecracker-style or with a pleated finish. Or, use several layers of tissue paper with a pleated finish at the bottom and a firecracker finish at the top, as you might wrap a wine bottle (see the following section).

An assortment of ways to wrap a round object. Note the diverse styles — tailored (pleats on the ends), fancy (firecracker finishes), whimsical (strips wrapped around the spheres), and unusual (the round object in the "ribbon cage").

Bottles of Wine

How many times have you brought a bottle of wine to some-one's home and wondered how you might have wrapped it more interestingly or festively? When it comes to wrapping wine bottles, most people are so concerned with the shape that they don't even worry about the embellishments on the package. Here are a few thoughts:

• Keep the wine bottle in the brown bag you receive at the wine store, but dress up the bag with glue-on stars, stickers, and a bow.

• Wrap layers of different-colored tissue paper around the bottle, treating it like a cylinder. Use a pleated finish at the bottom and a firecracker finish at the top; leave the top as is, or snip the tissue with scissors to make fringe. (*See Color Plate 7.*)

• Lay out several layers of tissue paper in different colors and place them over each other at different angles; bring up all the layers around the bottle, creating a big flourish of paper projecting upward, and tie with crimping ribbon.

• Purchase or make a decorated cloth sack, with a gather or drawstring at the neck; the sack can be an extra gift.

• Present the gift in a wicker wine-pouring stand, thus changing its shape; put the entire assembly in a box.

• "Plant" the bottle of wine in a flower pot.

• Dress up the bottle like a clown, an animal, or even a space-ship.

• Use lots of colored tissue paper to engulf the wine bottle in a shopping bag.

A variety of unusual, distinctive ways to wrap a bottle of wine.

Other Unusually Shaped Gifts

Most items that have unusual shapes also have other built-in problems. For example, consider a tennis racket and an umbrella. In a way, each could be wrapped as a rectangle—although the umbrella would need a good deal of tissue paper first for padding. With the tennis racket, basically the same problem exists.

Here's a list of items that sometimes pose problems when they have to be wrapped:

baseball bat	kiddy car
baseball glove	kitchen utensils
baton	lacrosse sticks
bicycle rack	lawn mower
bird feeder	mailbox
birdhouse	musical instrument
colander	rolling pin
desk or pole lamp	skis
fencing equipment	statuary
fireplace equipment	stroller
flower pot (with or without a plant)	telephone
football	tennis racket
gift basket of goodies	tools
golf clubs	umbrella
hamper	weathervane
high chair	

First of all, try to locate a box that can contain such items. If you have nothing suitable at home, then see if your local hardware, liquor, appliance, toy, and kiddy shop have any spare boxes.

Second, wrap the gift in mountains of tissue paper or newspaper. Make a support for it any way you can—sheets of corrugated cardboard, for example. After you've formed it into a more manageable shape, you should be able to wrap it more easily.

Third, consider wrapping the gift in a large, oversized plastic bag (clear or tinted) with decorative stickers on the outside.

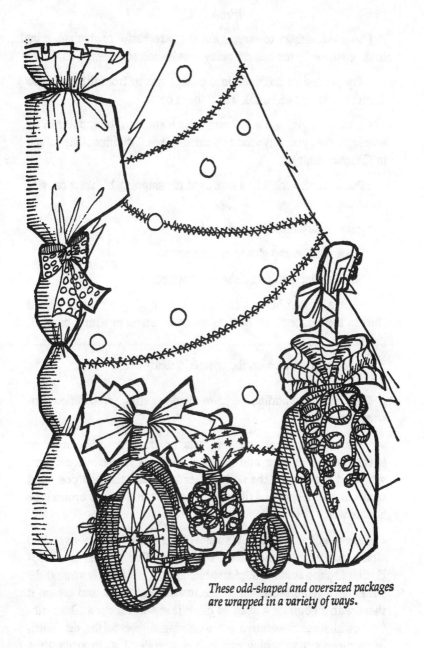

*These odd-shaped and oversized packages
are wrapped in a variety of ways.*

Use a subterfuge to wrap gifts that are easily recognizable by their shape or by the box that they usually come in:

• Try putting an umbrella into a large carton from the florist, so that the recipient will think it is a dozen roses.

• Instead of giving a handkerchief in a standard box, put it in an envelope that you have made yourself (see Traditional Envelope in Chapter Four).

• Put a tennis racket in a box used for shipping blankets or winter coats.

• Put a record album in a china box.

• Place mittens and gloves in shirt boxes.

• Stash a wine bottle in a shoe or boot box.

• Hide a gift within a gift, such as packaging a necktie with a shirt in the shirt box, or have a baseball packed in with a baseball glove.

• Place a wristwatch on the wrist of a teddy bear.

Here are a few additional ideas for decorating some difficult-to-wrap items:

• Festoon the wheel of a bicycle or tricycle with ribbon or streamers woven over and under the spokes of the wheels. Pull wrapping paper over the seat, gather it around the seat post, and secure it with a spray of ribbons. Tie an enormous bow around the handlebars.

• For a guitar or similar musical instrument, use an oversized cloth, such as those mentioned in Chapter Two (a painter's dropcloth, old shower curtain, picnic blanket), and gather it around the guitar. Bring the fabric up to the instrument's neck and secure it there with ribbon or a strip of cloth that will function like a ribbon. Add some decorative gift wrapping ribbon to the tie. Then, using more gift wrapping ribbon, spiral coils of it up around the neck of the guitar and tie in a bow there.

• For a pole lamp or other tall object, like skis, use an extra-large piece of fabric that is tall enough for the object and wrap it around the gift. Secure it at intervals with tiny pieces of ribbon, and at one point with a large bow.

Oversized Objects

Good things don't always come in small packages. Sometimes they come in giant, unwieldy crates. With a little help, you can turn these behemoths into nicely wrapped presents. It is important to remember that you cannot wrap these packages as you would wrap normal rectangles or squares. In many instances, you can merely make the suggestion of a wrapping on the carton. With many small touches, however, you can help make a stereo, bicycle, or piece of furniture look a bit more festive.

To wrap oversized boxes, use wrapping paper from a roll and envelop the package. Here are some suggestions for other boxes that you might have trouble deciding how to wrap.

• For a microwave oven, broiler, or rotisserie, cut out recipes from magazines and plaster them all over the box, as if they were foreign travel stickers. Festoon a few wooden kitchen implements on the top of the box with a huge bow.

• For a new television, bedeck the sides of the box with program listings and attach a TV magazine with a bow.

• Envelop the package in computer print-out paper; then make a large-scale drawing on the paper, using watercolors or markers, or paste on large geometric shapes cut from construction paper.

• Wrap a lawn mower in movers' pads, painters' dropcloths, or several old shower curtains. Decorate the surface and tie a bow at the end of the handle.

• Drape old tablecloths over a piano and pin large, cut-out musical notes onto the fabric. Use construction paper or fabric to make the notes.

• Roll strips of crepe paper streamers around the armature of a bicycle; tie bows of crepe paper streamers to all the spokes.

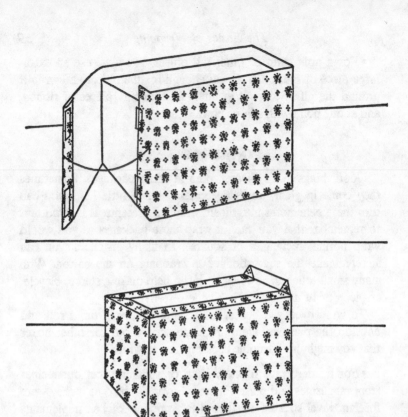

Wrapping an oversized box. Cover it in sections, with pieces of paper. Sometimes you may need to wrap only five of the six sides.

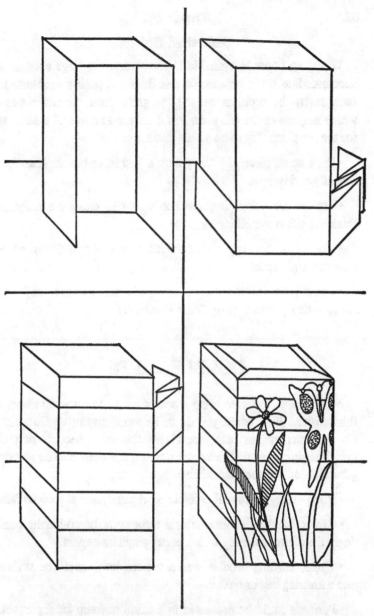

Computer print-out paper (on long, continuous rolls) can be used to wrap very large boxes. Decorate the outside of the box with large designs, like these tall flowers.

Undersized Objects

Wrapping paper is available in sheets that are large enough to accommodate small objects, so this does not pose a problem. In such cases, the problem can be the gift's sheer miniature size—which may make the gift seem less dramatic and less of a surprise for the recipient. Try to be a little inventive:

• Pin a small piece of jewelry onto a T-shirt or blouse; then fold it neatly and wrap it.

• Put theater tickets inside a box that will make the recipient think the gift is something else.

• Use a box that suggests it contains gloves or a tie for an envelope containing money.

• Use a gaily colored shopping bag and lots of tissue paper to nestle a tiny present. (*See Color Plate 17.*)

DOUBLE GIFTS

Next time you plan to bring a box of candy to someone's home, think twice. What could you do to be more inventive? Gifts that are presented within other containers, that soon become part of the gift, are one of the nicest ways to wrap a present. The second gift need not be expensive, either:

• Bring candy in a small ceramic bowl purchased at a crafts fair.

• Give a batch of croissants in a terra cotta bread-baking pan; tie up the entire assembly with a pretty gingham napkin.

• Yarns, knitting needles, and a pattern book could be stuffed into a knitting bag or basket.

• Perfume could be presented in a small makeup kit for travel.

• Desk supplies for the new writer (or a friend who gets a new job) could be wrapped in a desk organizer.

• A pair of pajamas for a child could be given in a pajama bag.

• A sewing kit could contain all the necessary notions a beginner needs.

• Exotic spices could be put into the empty jars of a spice rack.

• A glass cruet set could be given with a bottle of raspberry vinegar and imported oil.

• A tea drinker would welcome a teapot brimming over with a supply of interesting gourmet teas.

• A fountain pen (or pen and pencil set) could be tucked into a box with personalized stationery.

• A new pipe, along with a few selections of tobacco, could be concealed in a humidor.

• For the new ten-speed bike owner, a sturdy wicker basket might contain a set of bike repair tools, trouser clips, reflectors, and maybe a book of bike routes.

• A set of flatware for the bride and groom could be wrapped in a pair of elegant napkins, festooned with a gay bow, and presented in a decorated shopping bag.

• Other unusual containers you might consider for your gifts include an ice bucket, a flower pot, a pot/bowl/strainer from the kitchen, a wastepaper basket, a scrub pail, a child's brightly colored sand pail, or even a picnic basket.

With some thought, you will be able to look at all kinds of items stored away around your home and realize that they might make good containers for gift wrapping. But for those times when only a box—and an unusual one, at that—will do, the next chapter features information on how to make your own.

CHAPTER FOUR

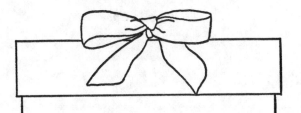

Making Customized Boxes, Bags, Envelopes

$\mathcal{F}$or those occasions when you can't find (or buy) the box or bag that you need for a gift, or for those times that you want a really special personalized container, you will want to make one yourself.

Making such containers is very easy once you have a basic pattern as a guide. The most difficult part of constructing these containers is the planning—determining your needs, selecting the right cardboard or paper, and enlarging the basic pattern. The actual processes of folding and pasting the paper are simple.

An added benefit to making your own container is that you can present a completely coordinated present. Many contemporary gift wrap manufacturers currently market matching bows and papers; but you will be able to go beyond that to make a box, card or gift tag, and other decorations to coordinate a complete wrapping theme. Add to this your selection of tissue paper, and you'll have a creation worthy of a picture.

CUSTOMIZING EXISTING CONTAINERS WITH FABRIC OR PAPER

The easiest way to customize a box is to cover an existing one with selected fabric or paper. The simplest type to cover is a heavy cardboard box that has a separate lid. And no matter what shape of box you use, make sure it has firm sides.

Think about your choice of paper or fabric and how you will employ it. You can cover the bottom of a box in one fabric and cover the lid with a contrasting fabric. Or you can use a solid-colored material on one part of the box and a matching stripe or print on the other.

Covering a Rectangular or Square Box

Even if both the top and the bottom of the box are of the same depth, they will not be covered in precisely the same fashion, since they serve different functions. Once covered, the lid should have as few seams on top as possible. The bottom of the box can have many seams or raw edges, since that part will not show.

The lid and the bottom of the box are covered as easily in paper as in fabric, and the same directions apply for both, with a slight exception. With fabric, you will need spray adhesive. With paper, you can use a spray adhesive meant for paper, or simply apply the paper and then use double-stick tape to adhere the edges.

Paper is thinner than fabric. For convenience' sake, do not use a bulky fabric such as a brocade or heavy velvet. Stick to lightweight sheers or cottons. As you can imagine, a lid that fits snugly will probably be tight once it has been covered with fabric—particularly when there are folds and tucks of fabric inside the lid.

Materials:
Box to be covered
Selected fabric (or paper)*
Newspaper for work surface
Fabric shears (paper shears)
Spray adhesive for fabric (double-stick tape for paper)
Ruler or yardstick
Paint scraper (optional)
Glue stick
Small, sharp trimming scissors

To cover the bottom of the box with fabric (or paper):

1. Determine the amount of fabric necessary to cover the out-side by wrapping a measuring tape around the four sides of the box. Add to that measurement 3 inches: 1 inch to allow for a "hem" on the raw edge, and 2 inches to allow for overlap.

2. Measure the height of the box; add 2 inches to turn over the top edge of the box, and 2 inches to turn under to the bottom of the box.
   (*Note:* This allowance will not work with tiny jewelry boxes, since they are not large enough to allow for this amount of excess.)

3. Cover your work surface with newspaper. Cut the fabric and spray the wrong side of it with glue. Start applying the fabric, as shown, 1 inch past the corner edge. Be certain that the fabric is centered on the box, so that there are 2 inches along both the top and bottom edges. Smooth the fabric along the surface as you work with your hand (or the paint scraper, if desired). When you return to the start-ing point, overlap the fabric, and make a 1-inch hem. Use the glue stick to adhere the hemmed 1-inch strip to the box.

---

* *The method presented in these instructions will be easier to work through with fabric (and will probably be more successful) than with paper—but it will work for both.*

4. Using the trimming scissors, cut the fabric at each corner, as shown, from the edge to the top of the box. Cut in a straight line down to the top edge of the box. Fold each of these four flaps down along the top edge of the box, inside it.

5. Repeat Step #4 on the bottom edge of the box, but do not cut straight slits; instead, trim away slight V-shaped wedges at each corner.

6. To cover the outside bottom of the box, cut a piece of fabric 1 inch less all around than the measurement of the bottom. Adhere to the box with the spray adhesive. Now, the entire outside of the bottom part of the box is covered.

7. To cover the inside of the bottom of the box, you will need a strip of fabric to run the perimeter of the interior. Measure the length of the necessary fabric and add 2 inches to that measurement. Then measure the height of the box, and subtract 1 inch from that measurement. Cut the fabric to size and adhere, starting 1 inch from the corner, so that the finished edge ends up in the corner.

8. To finish the inside of the box, measure the inside bottom of the box and cut a piece of fabric to size. Adhere it to the box.

To cover the lid of a rectangular or square box:

9. Measure the length, width, and height of the lid. Allow for additional fabric, to turn under to the inside of the lid.

10. Cut the necessary fabric and use spray adhesive on it. Center the top of the lid on the fabric by placing the fabric wrong (sprayed) side up, and placing the lid on it.

11. To allow for contouring at the corners, cut at the four points, as shown. Bring the fabric around the two corners and trim away the excess that may overlap. Repeat at the other end of the box. Bring up the two flaps. Repeat the procedures used in Step #4 to finish the edges.

12. To cover the inside of the top of the box, follow the procedures outlined in Steps #7 and 8.

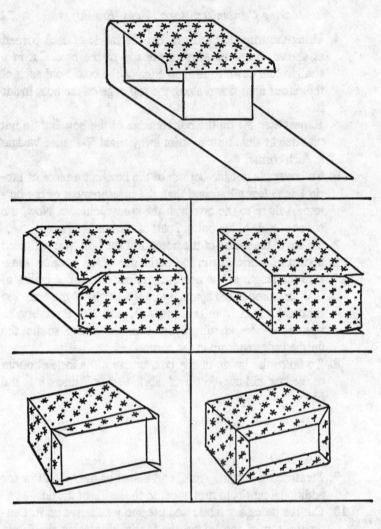

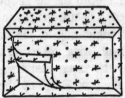

Covering the outside of a rectangular or square box with fabric or paper.

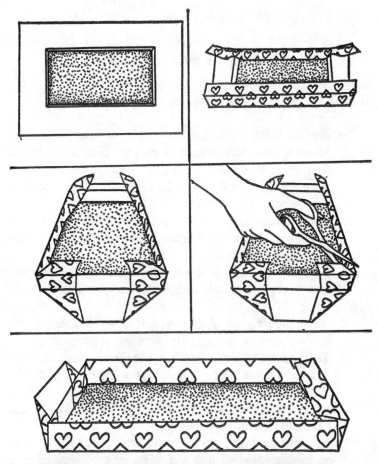

Covering the lid of a rectangular or square box with fabric or paper. Be sure that the material is carefully joined at an angle at the corners of the box, or there will be too much bulk for the lid to fit comfortably.

Covering a Round or Oval Box

Materials:
Same as for the rectangular or square box

To cover the bottom of the box with fabric (or paper):

1. Measure the circumference of the box; then add 2 inches for overlap and 1 inch for a hem. Measure the height and allow for a 2-inch excess at the top and a 2-inch excess at the bottom.
2. Cover the box as you did in Step #3 of "Covering a Rectangular or Square Box," hemming and overlapping the fabric in the same fashion.
3. To turn under the excess fabric on the bottom, you will have to clip the curves, as shown, in order to make the fabric fit.
4. Along the rim edge of the box, turn down the fabric to the inside of the box, occasionally clipping it as necessary.
5. To cover the bottom of the box, use the box itself as a pattern for a circle. Draw it on the wrong side of the fabric, and cut it out about ½ inch smaller than the pattern line, using pinking shears, if possible. Spray with adhesive and adhere to the bottom of the box.
6. To cover the inside of the box, follow the same procedures outlined in Steps #7 and 8 of "Covering a Rectangular or Square Box."

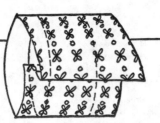

Covering a cylinder with fabric or paper. Clip the material along both curved edges.

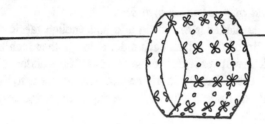

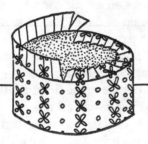

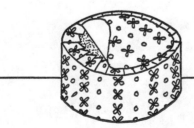

To cover the lid of a round or oval box:

7. Measure the diameter of the lid and add enough fabric to cover the lip of the lid on each side. Add another inch to that, which will provide for a ½-inch turn-under all around. Cut the circle of fabric needed and adhere it to the lid, as outlined in Step #10 of "Covering a Rectangular or Square Box."

8. Clip the curves all around the edge, as shown. Adhere the fabric to the lip of the lid and then turn under the ½-inch excess all the way around.

9. Finish the inside of the lid as in Steps #7 and 8 of "Covering a Rectangular or Square Box."

10. Around the outside of the lip of the lid, run a band of ribbon or trimming to conceal any raw or sloppy edges. This will help hide the clipped fabric—particularly if it is solid-colored. If it is a print, the cutting will be less obvious.

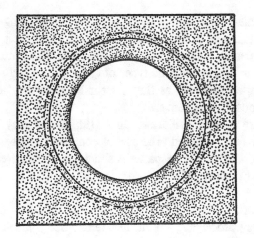

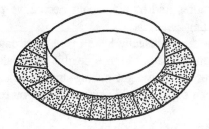

Covering the lid of a round container with fabric or paper. The circular edge will look neat and "finished" only if the covering material is clipped around the lip of the lid.

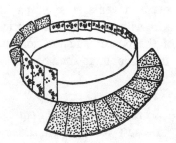

MAKE-YOUR-OWN GIFT CONTAINERS

In this section there are patterns for constructing several types of containers. All are made simply by folding the patterns as indicated, and gluing the flaps as marked. The patterns here are guides to making specific types of containers. They are not meant to be used precisely as they appear here, as they are too small. They must be scaled to size.

These patterns are drawn on a grid, so that they can be easily enlarged and adapted. The size of container you'll want will vary from gift to gift; these patterns should serve as an easy reference for your future needs.

Materials:

Before proceeding any further, familiarize yourself with the materials that are available for you to work with. Look at the heavy boards in art supply stores and inquire about decorative papers and imported bookbinding materials.

Envelopes and bags do not usually have to be as strong as a box; therefore, they can be made of more flexible materials. For more demanding chores, a lightweight oaktag—malleable enough to fold, yet stronger than paper—would work well for you to construct such items.

Boxes should be made from a medium-weight poster board or mat board, available in stationery or art supply stores. There are several advantages to poster boards: they are a good weight to work with; are available in bright colors; have color on both sides of the board; and are sold in large sheets, enabling the construction of large-sized boxes.

Scoring, Cutting, and Folding:

Because you will be working with heavier-weight materials than just traditional wrapping paper, you will need special tools for cutting. As mentioned in Chapter One, never use scissors to cut heavy papers and boards. This is a job for a mat knife.

First of all, work on a clean, debris-free surface. Use a cork-backed ruler, at least 15 inches long, against which to make your cuts. The cork prevents the ruler from sliding; the metal provides a solid edge to work and cut against.

To make a clean cut, use a long, swift stroke of the mat knife, with enough pressure to go all the way through the mat board. To score the board, do not apply as much pressure; you merely want to make a channel, not cut through it. Always work with a sharp blade.

Scoring is etching out a channel in a heavy board as a guideline for a fold. To get a heavy poster board to fold easily, use your cork-backed ruler and cut partway through the thick board with your mat knife, creating a line for the fold to follow.

Mountain and Valley Folds:

There are two types of folds that you will need to understand before undertaking the patterns in this section. To visualize them, take a piece of scrap paper and fold it into an accordion—a set of even up-and-down pleats. Place it on a flat surface. You will notice that there are folds that are raised (that come up toward you, as mountains) and folds that are lowered (that recede from you, as valleys). In the traditional Japanese art of origami, or paper folding, that is what these folds are called; therefore, we will refer to them in that same way.

The mountain side of a fold forces the paper at the point of the fold to "stretch," while the valley fold forces it to "compress." Heavyweight cardboard, therefore, must have the benefit of scoring, to enable it to stretch around corners to create a fold.

All folds are indicated in the patterns that follow, using traditional Japanese identification. Almost every fold line made with material heavier than oaktag will have to be scored first.

• Mountain folds are designated by a broken line (or series of dashes).

• Valley folds are marked by a line composed of dots.

• Cutting lines are solid, unbroken lines.

• The depth of the scoring will depend on the weight of the paper.

• Patterns are presented with either the inside or the outside of the container showing, depending on which illustrates more material and makes the construction process simpler to execute.

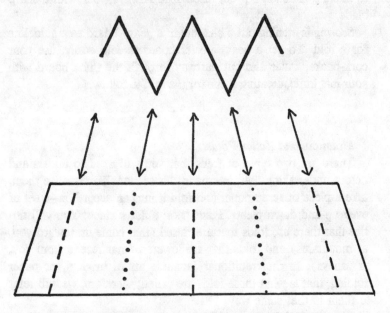

Mountain folds are indicated on grid patterns by broken lines; valley folds, by a series of dots.

Covering Homemade Containers with Fabric or Paper

Once you have cut a desired pattern from oaktag or cardboard and have made the necessary scoring cuts, you are ready to construct the item. If, however, you want to cover the container with fabric or paper, now is the time to do it—not later, after it is already constructed.

The big advantage to covering the items you make with fabric or paper at this point (rather than after théy are built) is that they are still basically flat. It is much easier to cover a flat item than a three-dimensional one. This way, the inside and the outside of the container can be covered with a minimum of effort.

After you have covered the container with the fabric or paper that you've chosen, you are then ready to follow the specific instructions for constructing that container. The materials that you will need are the same as those listed in the section "Customizing Existing Containers with Fabric or Paper." (Assume here that you are working with fabric.)

1. Cut out the oaktag according to the pattern's shape. Read through all the directions and make all the required folds, flexing the oaktag into its ultimate form. *Do not do any gluing at this time, regardless of the pattern instructions.*
2. Flatten the oaktag again and place it on the wrong side of the fabric. Use the oaktag shape as a guide and trace around its perimeter with a pencil or tailor's chalk. Add an extra inch all around this first drawing, and use the second, larger drawing as the cutting guide.
3. Cut a second piece of fabric the same size as the first. Set the second piece aside.
4. Working on a large area covered with newspaper, spray the oaktag (not the fabric) with the adhesive, on the side of the oaktag that will be the outside of the container. Hold the fabric centered over the sprayed side of the oaktag base, with the right side of the fabric facing up. Lower the fabric to the oaktag and press the center of the fabric down to the oaktag base, contouring it to the folds in the pattern. Force the oaktag base into its pattern shape, molding the fabric over it.

   (*Note:* It is important when you cover a fold of the oaktag base that the fabric covering it is folded to the same shape. Therefore, the fabric must be worked slowly and carefully over the oaktag, as you fold it. Since the spray adhesive allows for repositioning, you will have little problem working in sections. The covering around each fold should be executed separately, as you make that fold with the oaktag.)

5. Trim away all excess fabric from the perimeter of the oaktag base, using trimming scissors.
6. Repeat the procedures outlined in Steps #4 and 5, to cover the other side (inside) of the container.
7. When the entire container is covered, you can follow the specific instructions to construct the container to its finished shape.

In addition to the required materials listed in the above step-by-step description, you may also need the following supplies to construct your own containers:

X-acto knife (for detail cutting)
paper, pinking, or fabric shears
ruler, measuring tape, yardstick, metal cutting ruler, T-square
glue stick, rubber cement, white glue
wax paper
hole puncher

(*Note:* Whenever you are enlarging a pattern and drawing it on the paper or cardboard that you will be using for construction, always draw the pattern on the wrong side of the paper or cardboard.)

Traditional Envelope

This is an ideal container to enclose the gift of a scarf, set of handkerchiefs, a picture, a T-shirt, even a thin book. This envelope can easily be put to use again, after the gift is removed.

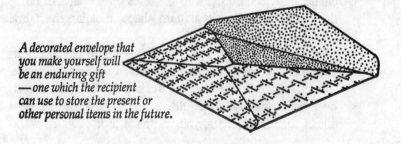

A decorated envelope that you make yourself will be an enduring gift — one which the recipient can use to store the present or other personal items in the future.

1. Cut out the pattern.
2. Make all the folds as indicated on the pattern, without doing any gluing.
3. *To assemble:* Fold Flap A in toward the center and then fold Flap B in to meet it. Flap B will overlap A slightly. Glue together at that point, being careful not to allow the glue to seep out of the join to the inside. If this occurs, you can put a sheet of wax paper inside the envelope to protect it. Next, bring up Flap C, overlapping Flaps A and B, where they are joined. Fold Flap D. Allow the glue to dry. Place the envelope under a book while it is drying, to help flatten it. Place a sheet of wax paper in between the book and the envelope.
4. *To keep the envelope closed:* a) cut a small slit in the envelope to insert Flap D; or b) attach (sew, glue, or staple) a ribbon near the point of Flap D, which can encircle the envelope and tie at the front.

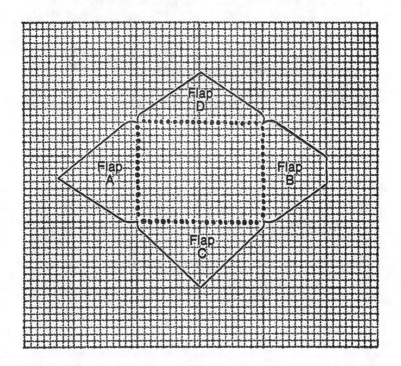

Simple Business-style Envelope

This style of envelope resembles a manila envelope used in offices. If you change the dimensions of the basic envelope, you can make this vertical shape into a horizontal or square one—the latter would be ideal to hold a record album.

1. Cut out the pattern and make the folds as indicated.
2. *To assemble:* Fold Side B up to meet Side A, so that they meet squarely. Fold Flaps C and D over onto Side B; glue both flaps in place.
3. Fold Flap E as directed and place the finished envelope under a book while drying, as in Step #3 for the Traditional Envelope.
4. *To keep the envelope closed:* Cut a slit in the body of Side B, as indicated, so that you can insert Flap E into it.

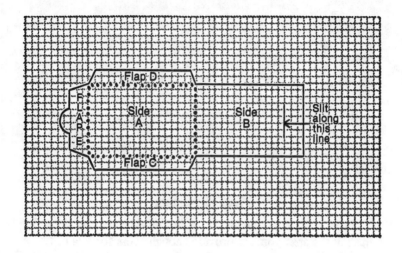

Flap D

F
L
A
P
E

Side
A

Side
B

Slit
along
this
line

Flap C

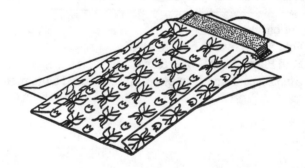

This style of envelope is perfect to enclose relatively flat presents. If you change the shape a bit, you'll have a container for a record album.

Plain Paper Bag

This is a good wrapping for a hard-to-box article since, by adjusting the size, you can provide enough room for lots of tissue paper, cushioning, odd shapes, etc. The bag can be simply gathered at the top, or the edges can be neatly turned down, and stick-on decorations added. (*See Color Plate 17.*)

1. Cut out the pattern.
2. Fold Side B over to meet Side A.
3. Fold Flaps C and D over Side B.
4. Glue Flaps C and D in place. Allow to dry before putting to use.

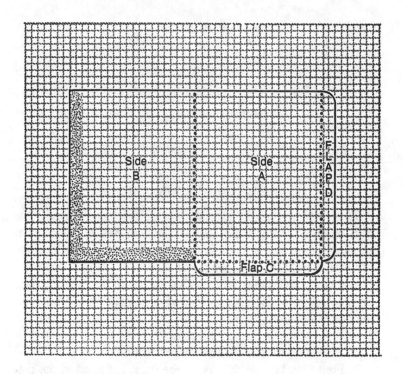

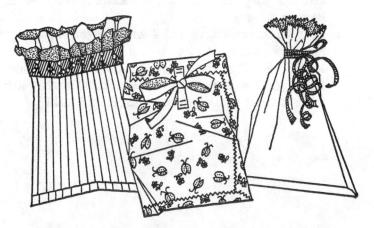

This bag can be made with or without a flap at the top. Gather the "neck" of the bag and you'll have an entirely different finished product.

Square Box with Attached Lid

This pattern is highly adaptable for different-sized gifts. It has flaps on both the top and bottom of the box, making it somewhat stronger than a box without any reinforcement. The flaps overlap, but you can change their length so that they just meet, or completely cover each other. You can also alter the length of the flaps on the bottom of the box, so that when they are glued together, the box is stabilized.

1. Flex every fold line to start forming the box.
2. Fold Flap G onto Side A, at the point indicated in the pattern, making sure that it is on the inside of the box. Glue, and hold in place with tape, if necessary. Allow to dry. Remove the tape.
3. Fold the bottom Flaps J and K and close the bottom cover Flap E. Repeat for the top, folding Flaps H and I, and the lid, Flap F. If the bottom and top lids do not sit properly against the box, make a tiny slit as indicated on the pattern in the corner of both sides of each lid (Flaps E and F).

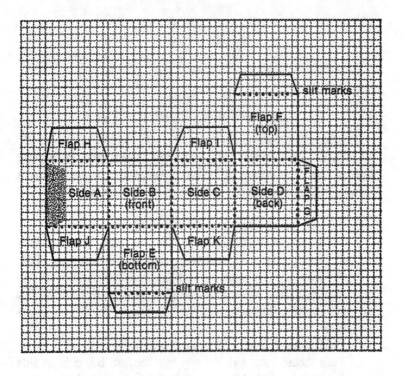

Flap F (top)

slit marks

Flap H   Flap I

Flap J   Flap K

Side A   Side B (front)   Side C   Side D (back)   FLAP G

Flap E (bottom)

slit marks

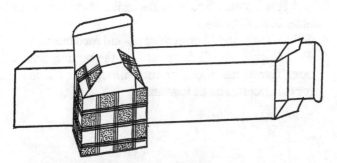

This kind of box can be used for just about all your gift wrapping needs, since it is adaptable in shape and size.

Reinforced Box with Ribbon Ties

This box, like the one above, can be adapted in endless ways to make a tall, thin rectangle; or a short, squat one; or a large square. The holes on top of the box allow you to feed a ribbon or yarn tie closure through them, and then around the box.

1. Give all the fold lines a preliminary flex.
2. Fold Flaps B and C firmly, so that you bring them in to Side A (the bottom) and over it. See that they fit snugly over Side A. Glue them in place. Secure the outside with tape to hold all the sides in place while the glue dries. Note also that this action forces three sides of the box (K, D, and E) into position.
3. Fold Sides H and I in toward each other until they meet. Push them forward all the way into the box, bringing up Side J. Note that Side H covers Side D on the inside of the box and Side I covers Side E on the inside of the box. Glue both Sides H and I in place.
4. Fold Flaps L and M downward toward each other.
5. Fold Flaps F and G downward, as the outside cover of the box. Thread the ribbon or cord through the punched holes for the closure, and tie together.

punch
hole
here

Flap L | Flap F (top) | Flap M

Side D | Side K | Side E

Flap B | | Flap C

Side A (bottom)

Side H | Side J | Side I

Flap G (top)

punch
hole
here

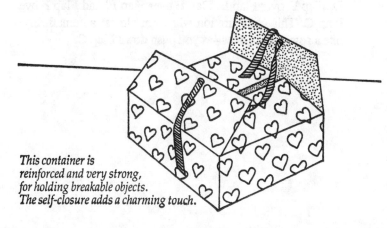

*This container is
reinforced and very strong,
for holding breakable objects.
The self-closure adds a charming touch.*

Flower Box

The closure of this decorative box looks somewhat like the petals of a flower. If you decorate the box with cut-outs in the shapes of flowers, you can make it look even more like a blossoming plant. For example, use construction paper to make "fringed grass" to attach along the bottom edge of the box. Add some tall stems that go up toward the top of the box, with petals on the ends. Make one stem go all the way to the top, so that the closure becomes the flower for that stem.

1. Make all the valley folds as indicated on the pattern.
2. Very carefully score the four lines marked on the mountain sides of the folds.
3. Form the box by gluing Flaps A and B in place, as indicated on the pattern.
4. Create the bottom of the box by gluing the four bottom flaps: First, glue G to I; then fold and glue H to G and I. Then fold J over and glue it to G, H, and I.
5. Form the top of the box by folding down Flap C over Flap D, Flap D over Flap E, Flap E over Flap F, and Flap F over Flap C. This configuration will form almost automatically—like a row of dominoes—as you push down Flap C.

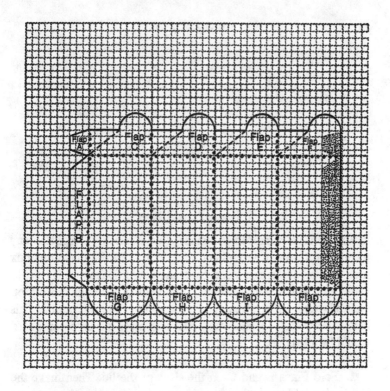

Flap A
Flap C
Flap D
Flap E
Flap F
FLAP B
Flap G
Flap H
Flap I
Flap J

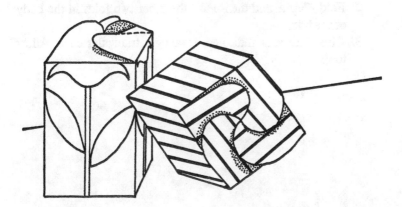

This "flower box" surely holds a special gift. The outside looks especially appropriate when it is made up to look like a flower.

Cone-shaped Box

This unusually shaped container is an especially delightful way to present a present at holiday time. You can even make this box look like an ice cream cone by constructing it from beige paper (with a cross-hatch design on it), and adding two pompons on top —a fluffy pink for strawberry and a creamy white for vanilla. This box is very easy to construct, and one piece of shirt cardboard would be adequate.

1. Fold Flaps B and C on the sides of the lid. Then make the third fold marked on the lid, between it and the body of the box.
2. Fold Flap A and then make the other two folds in the body of the box.
3. Glue Flap A as indicated, forming a triangular cone. Allow to dry.

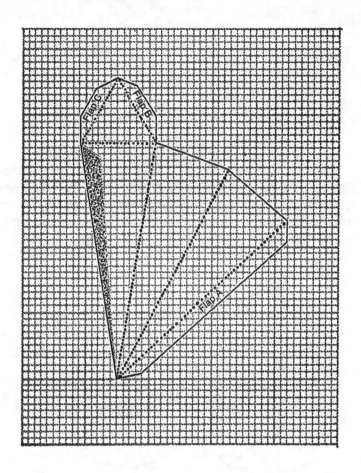

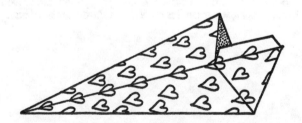

This cone-shaped box can be packed with jelly beans, licorice, or other small confections. Or fill a lot of these boxes with small gifts and hang them as ornaments on a Christmas tree.

Torpedo Box

This is a wonderful container in which to present fresh flowers (like an orchid for Mother's Day), an assortment of scented soaps and essences, a collection of smaller gifts, a pipe and tobacco for Dad, etc. Notice that one end of the torpedo is flat, with the paper pleated, just as the cylinder shapes are in Chapter Three. The other end is softly gathered with a ribbon. (*See Color Plate 15.*)

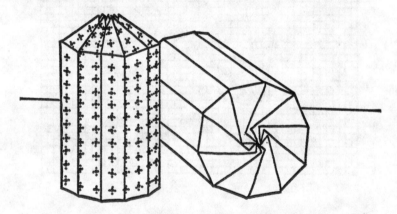

This unusual box is a versatile container for gifts and can be used over and over again when it is made with a sturdy cardboard base.

There are two variations for finishing the top of the cylinder. They are presented in the patterns below; substitute either one for a different look. Pattern A further divides each closure flap of the pattern for the Torpedo Box (Flaps B through K) in half with a fold, and cuts the ends to points. Hence, the effect is a multi-folded starburst look. Pattern B does the opposite—it doubles the width of each flap and provides for a fold down the center of the flaps. The finished cylinder using this pattern edge also has a star-burst appearance, but with a much more tailored look.

Also remember that you can use any of the three finishing techniques on *both* ends of the Torpedo Box, instead of a pleated finish on the bottom as shown in the pattern on page 99.

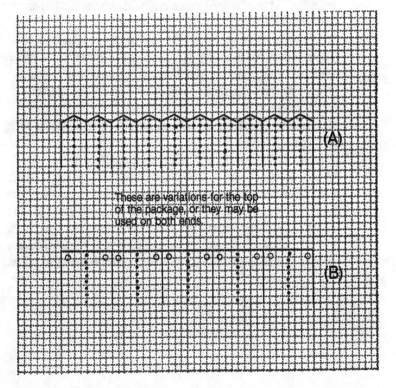

These are variations for the top of the package, or they may be used on both ends.

1. Score the indicated mountain folds, which will help make the pleats.
2. Make all the valley folds, as marked.
3. Form the cylinder shape by temporarily taping Flap A in place.
4. Starting at the point where Flap A is taped to the cylinder, press the pleats down to a flat position on the bottom of the cylinder. (If they do not move easily, then you must open up the cylinder and score them a little better.)
5. Remove the tape, position Flap A carefully, and glue it in place. Allow them to dry. To hold the cylinder in its shape while the glue is drying, use either snippets of tape along the seam, or several ribbons or strings tied gently around the circumference.
6. Rework the pleats on the bottom of the cylinder, gluing each in place.
7. Punch a hole in each of the ten closure Flaps B through K, as indicated. Thread a ribbon through them, going through each hole from the outside of the package to the inside. The flaps will automatically overlap each other as you pull the ribbon. Reinsert the end of the ribbon into the first hole, where the tail of the ribbon is, and then pull gently. Make a box to complete the closure and keep the fastening in place.

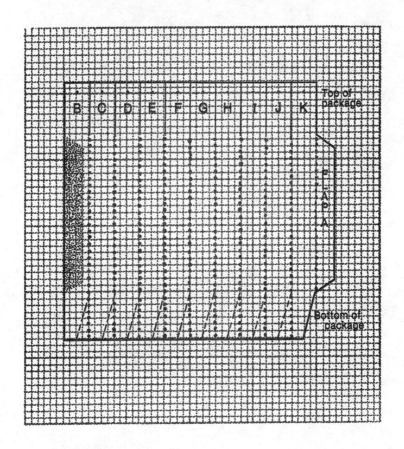

Now that you have worked your way through these patterns, you are probably pleased to see how easily you can create boxes for your presents—and interesting shaped boxes, at that. In the next chapter there are step-by-step instructions for making lovely bows to adorn your hand-made containers.

CHAPTER
FIVE

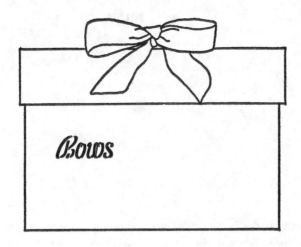

Bows

$\mathcal{N}$early everyone knows how to tie a bow, and the basic mechanics of looping, twisting, pulling, and securing the tie strings. The mechanical movements of tying a bow—just like tying shoe laces—are automatic, and such familiarity often causes us to make something less than the perfect bow. In fact, it is just as easy to create a great-looking bow as it is to make a merely passable one.

When you make a lot of bows from different types of material, you'll see just how many different effects you can achieve. Experiment with various kinds of ribbon found around the house, as well as with strips of paper, lengths of fabric, even string. Keep the length of the pieces consistent, but vary the width of the materials. You will observe that both the width and texture of the ribbon will affect the type of bow you get.

Some hints for making bows are included in this chapter, and none of them requires learning new skills. You simply have to refine the skills you have and plan ahead to utilize the most appropriate type of ribbon for the bow you are making.

Look at the bows in the accompanying illustration and notice how very different they are. Then think about the bows that you've seen at florist shops, or those manufactured by gift wrapping companies—they're all perfect. By using a few tricks known to the professionals—a little nip here, a secret tuck there, a separate piece of ribbon added on—you, too, can make flawless bows.

Some other tricks that you can use include "wiring" or starching bows so that they stand up crisp and tall; adding on individual ribbon pieces for "tails," so that the bow has a symmetric look; and "constructing" or building a bow, using wire at the center to coax a length of ribbon into a bow shape that remains firm and taut. The instructions in this chapter will show you how to employ some of these methods for making bows which can be attached to your gifts.

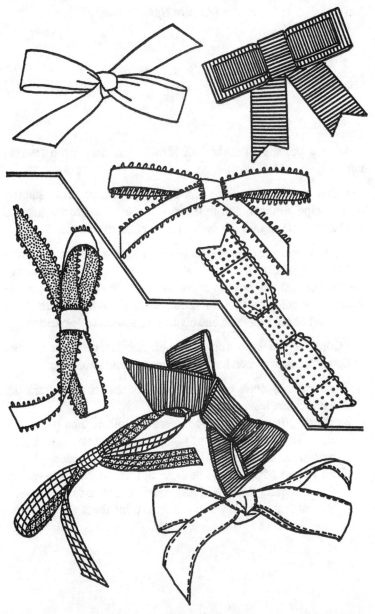

Here are a variety of bows made with approximately the same length of ribbon. Notice how different they all look. The bows on the top half were made by using techniques practiced by professionals. Those on the bottom half of the page were made in the casual way most of us usually tie bows — and they are a little weary-looking because of their construction.

As you prepare to make individual bows, here are a few reminders:

• Have all the necessary supplies handy—scissors, tape, stapler, wire or pipe cleaners, and thin twist-ties (used to secure the tops of plastic bags) or thin (⅛ inch wide) lengths of ribbon.

• Before you start, decide on the look that you want the package to have. Frilly? Tailored? What type of paper are you using? Would you like the bow to coordinate with the paper for a monochromatic color scheme, or should it be a bold departure from the paper? Should there be one big bow or several little ones?

• Consider the type and width of ribbon you want to use. Different types of ribbon have specific assets and liabilities:

Paper ribbons don't have the flexibility that cloth ribbons do, but they are less costly.

Synthetic gift wrapping ribbons are less pliant than paper ribbons. They also split apart easily, but sometimes that characteristic can be an asset—if you want to fringe the ends.

Cloth ribbons don't have the bounce that synthetics have, but they are quite stable and lush-looking. The ends may ravel a bit, but that shouldn't stop you from using them.

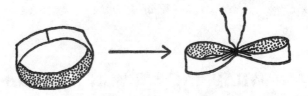

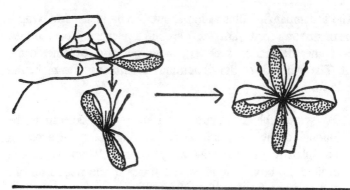

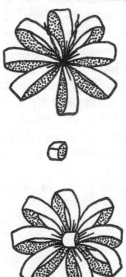

Here's an example of a beautiful bow, created the professional way. It is constructed from separate pieces of ribbon, held together with thin wire. You can do the same by using picture-hanging wire or even a plastic bag's twist-tie.

WRAPPING RIBBON AROUND
A PACKAGE

The accompanying illustration shows the basic steps to wrap a piece of ribbon (cord, yarn, etc.) around a package. You can then add another decoration such as a bow, pompon, or other ornament. The two ends of the ribbon may even be used to make the bow itself.

1. To wrap ribbon around a package, first determine the amount of ribbon you'll need, allowing plenty of excess if you plan to make a bow with the ends. Wrap the ribbon around the box, with about two thirds of the ribbon on one end and one third on the other end.
2. When both ends return to the top of the box, twist them around each other, as shown.
3. Using the longer ribbon tail, wrap the ribbon around the box in the other direction.
4. Return it (the ribbon with the long dashes in the drawing) to the top of the package and slip it under the twist on top of the package and then pull it taut.
5. Next, take the other ribbon tail (the one marked with dots) and slip it underneath the longer one, as shown.
6. Pull both ribbons taut.
7. Then make the knot (and bow, if you wish) as you normally would.

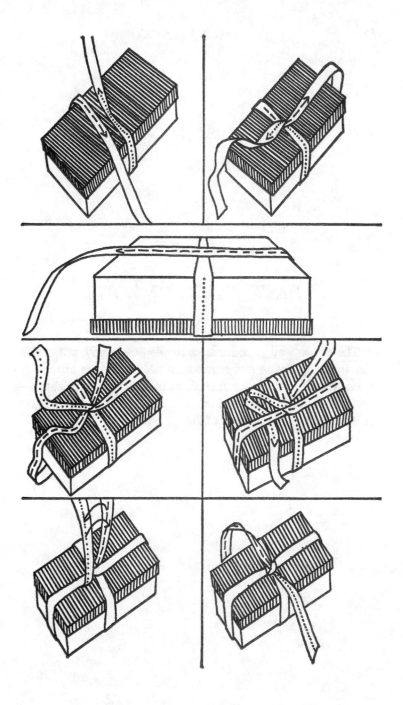

BASIC TYPES OF BOWS

Simple Bow

The easiest way to construct a simple bow is with self-sticking gift wrapping ribbon that requires no additional glue or tape. Instead, you can adhere separate pieces of ribbon to each other simply by moistening them, and create many diverse looks (as shown in the illustration at the start of this chapter).

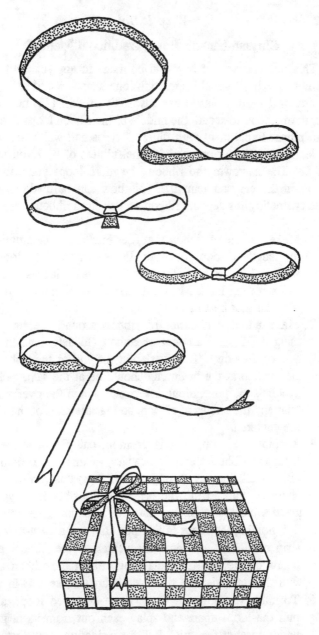

This bow is best made with a self-sticking synthetic gift-wrapping ribbon (the type that adheres to itself when it is moistened).

Chrysanthemum Bow (Traditional Method)

This popular type of bow can be made in any size; but when made properly, it should have only one shape—round and puffy.

You will need a plastic bag's twist-tie or thin (⅛ inch wide) length of ribbon to secure the middle of the ribbon loops in a taut, firm pinch. Experiment with different types and widths of ribbon to learn how much you need for the fullness of bow you prefer. (*Note:* The narrower the ribbon, the more loops you will need to fill in the chrysanthemum.) This bow can be made as easily with synthetic gift wrapping ribbon as with cloth ribbon.

1. Make a circle of ribbon that uses four times the amount for the length of loop you want. For example, if the loop you want is 3 inches high, then you will need 6 inches of ribbon to form each loop. Make the first circle of ribbon, overlapping the ends by 1 inch.
2. Make additional circles of ribbon around the first loop, using the desired amount of ribbon (to determine the fullness of the bow). The overlap at the end of the ribbon and the overlap at the beginning should be at the same point.
3. Holding the point along the circles where the overlaps are, "flatten" the circles of ribbon, so that the ends of the ribbon are centered.
4. Keeping the loops in this position, cut pie-shaped wedges from the ribbon along both edges, at this center point. Do not cut all the way through the ribbon; this cutting merely removes "bulk" from the center of the ribbons so you can make a puffy chrysanthemum with a minimum of effort.
5. Still holding the loops in this position, use a twist-tie or thin strip of ribbon to secure the center of the ribbon, at the points of the two triangular cuts. Pinch the ribbon tightly with the tie; twist the tie several times to keep it in place.
6. To make the bow out of all these anchored loops, simply pull the loops apart and splay each out from its neighbors with a twist of the wrist. Pull the inside loops out first, alternating right and left sides (working them in opposite directions).

7. Use a small pipe cleaner or piece of wire to attach the finished bow to the ribbon that is already on the package; or tape the bow directly to the box.

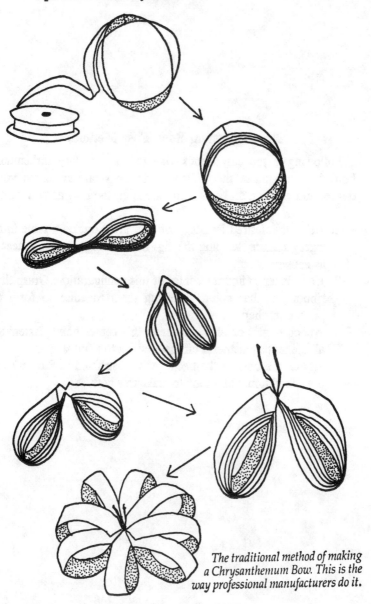

The traditional method of making a Chrysanthemum Bow. This is the way professional manufacturers do it.

Chrysanthemum Bow (Easy Method)

Following is the easy, quick way to make a chrysanthemum bow. You can make the "tails" of ribbon whatever length you desire, and you can make as many loops on the bow as you wish.

1. Using the desired length of ribbon, lay it out on a table in a zigzag pattern, keeping the zigs and the zags evenly spaced, as shown.
2. Use a ruler to find the center of this configuration. Grasp the ribbons at that point, squishing them together to form a puffy bow shape.
3. Attach a wire or pipe cleaner at this center point, fastening all the loops together. Puff the bow out to a full shape.
4. Attach the bow to the package, as instructed in Step #7 of the "Traditional Method" to make this bow.

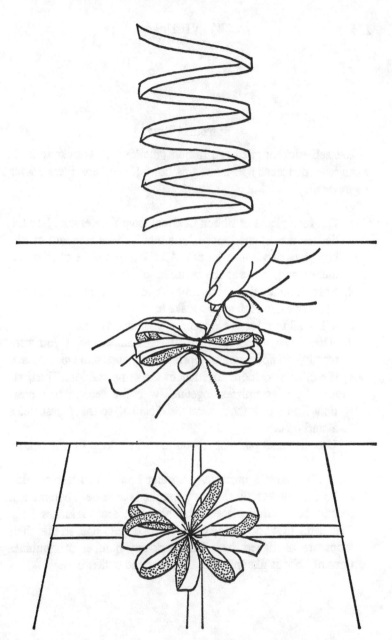

By using this shortcut method to make a Chrysanthemum Bow, you will still get a pretty, full "flower."

Starburst Bow

Use self-sticking gift wrap ribbon (the kind that sticks to itself when it is moistened) to make this bow. (*See Color Plate 16 for an example.*)

1. Cut four pieces of ribbon of equal length, determined by the desired size of the loops of the bow (a 9-inch length of ribbon gives two 2-inch loops). Also, cut one piece of ribbon 3 inches long, to use as the center loop.
2. Form individual circles with each of the 9-inch pieces of ribbon. Set aside each as you make it.
3. When all four loops are complete, "flatten" them.
4. Attach two loops together, at right angles, as if you were forming compass points—north, south, east, and west. Attach the other two loops together in the same fashion. Then, attach both assemblies together, with the second one positioned on top of the first on the diagonal, so that it resembles a starburst.
5. Use the small piece of ribbon to make a loop for the center.

(*Note:* To make a much larger, fuller bow in this fashion, first make the bow exactly as above. Set the bow aside. Then make a second bow, using pieces of ribbon that are 15 inches long. Center the first bow inside the second (larger) one, so that their loops are unaligned. You can work any number of combinations of ribbons like this to make fuller and puffier bows.)

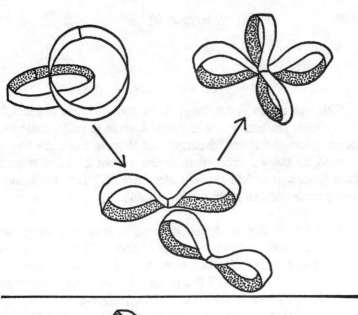

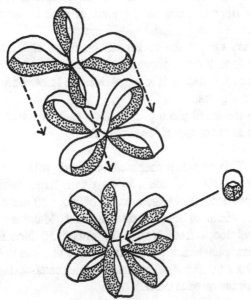

Although you can use any type of ribbon to make a Starburst Bow, it is made more easily with self-sticking gift wrap ribbon.

Pinwheel Bow

This type of bow is a variation of the Starburst Bow and is built in a similar fashion, with a slight twist—quite literally. Instead of forming circles that are "flattened" out to make loops, the bow is formed by *twisted* circles that, in the process of being twisted, form loops automatically. (*See Color Plate 16.*) This bow is most easily made with self-sticking gift wrap ribbon.

1. Cut two lengths of ribbon 9 inches long (providing two 2-inch loops). Cut two lengths of ribbon 18 inches long (an 18-inch length of ribbon gives two 4-inch loops). Also, cut one piece of ribbon 3 inches long, to use as the center loop.
2. Form figure eights with each of the 18-inch-long and 9-inch-long ribbons. Moisten the ends of each to secure them in place.
3. Attach two of the longer ribbon figure eights together, so they form a curly pinwheel, at right angles to each other.
4. Center the two smaller loops over the larger ones, and nestle them together.
5. Use the small piece of ribbon to make a round loop to attach as the center of the pinwheel.

(*Note:* This pinwheel shape can be made with any number of interior wheels. For example, start with large pinwheel loops, 24 inches each. Make the next set of loops 20 inches each, and set that circle of loops inside the first. Make a third set of pinwheel loops from lengths of ribbon 16 inches long, and when that pinwheel is constructed, place that one inside the second. Work the pinwheel circles at angles cater-cornered to each other, or inside each other.)

The Pinwheel Bow features a slight twist in the ribbon before the loops, resembling "figure eights," are formed.

Looped Bow

This bow is constructed from loops of ribbon. Each "flattened" circle of ribbon is made from a different length, and they are stacked on top of one another, graduating in size from the largest to the smallest. (*See Color Plate 16.*) Self-sticking gift wrap ribbons work the best.

1. Cut lengths of ribbon 14, 12, 10, 8, 6, and 4 inches. Starting from the largest piece of ribbon and proceeding to the smallest, have each form a circle; overlap the ends by ½ inch, and secure them. Keep the circles of ribbon in size order, so you don't make an error.

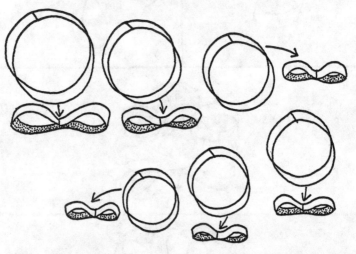

2. Starting with the largest circle and working to the smallest one, grasp the ribbon at the point of its overlapping fastening. Hold that point in one hand and pull the loop taut with your other hand so that, in effect, you are finding the halfway point of the rest of the ribbon. Join these two points by moistening the ribbon again. Then, stack the next larger ribbon on top of this one. Continue to pile these loops on top of each other, forming a bow with loops on each side of the center.

3. Use the smallest loop as the center circular loop; or you can cut another 2-inch length of ribbon and make a small loop for the center of the bow, to give it a more finished look. Wet the underside of the small loop to adhere it.

Another method to finish off the center of this style bow requires that you cut a small piece of ribbon, which should be slightly over twice the width of the ribbon. Hold the small piece of ribbon perpendicular to the bow assembly, so that it makes a tiny cross in the middle. Wrap the two ends of the tiny piece of ribbon around the assembly, so that they fold over to the bow's underside. Moisten both ends and secure them there.

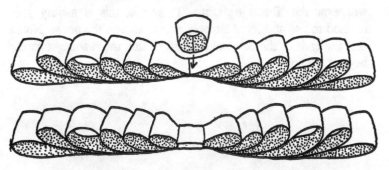

The Looped Bow is made with loops of graduated sizes. The center can be finished with a tiny loop placed on top of the center loop, or with a small piece of ribbon wrapped around the stacked loops.

"Pleated" Looped Bow

You can make many types of bows based on configurations of loops, secured by moistening the self-sticking ribbon and adhering it to itself. The first variation, the "Pleated" Looped Bow, is the type of bow that can go on endlessly, or it can be cut off at any point. As the illustration shows, the length of ribbon is simply folded back and forth over itself, creating loop upon loop. The loops on the outside part of the bow are larger than those on the lower portion of the bow. At each point of contact, the ribbon is moistened to hold it in place.

After the ribbon is folded back and forth a few times, the loops start to fan out. The "end" is reached whenever you want, or whenever the ribbon runs out. Therefore, this is a very good method to use up bits of leftover ribbon around the house. Notice that the ends of the bow are left cut, so that the raw edges extend beyond the bow.

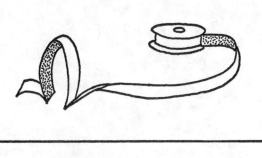

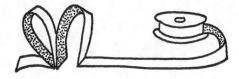

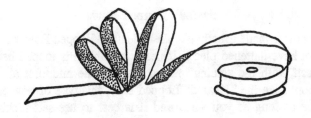

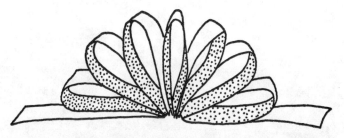

The easy-to-make "Pleated" Looped Bow consists of one continuous piece of ribbon folded back and forth over itself, with sharp creases at the center. Self-sticking gift wrapping ribbon works best; cloth ribbon could be used instead, but you'll need glue to hold the loops together and the creases won't have the same sharpness.

"Unpleated" Looped Bow

This bow is made exactly like the "Pleated" Looped Bow, but it does not have flattened pleats. Instead, the ribbon is looped back over itself, with the "gluing" taking place at the midpoint along each loop. Like the "Pleated" Looped Bow, this type of bow can be made as long as you wish, and it is best to use self-sticking ribbon.

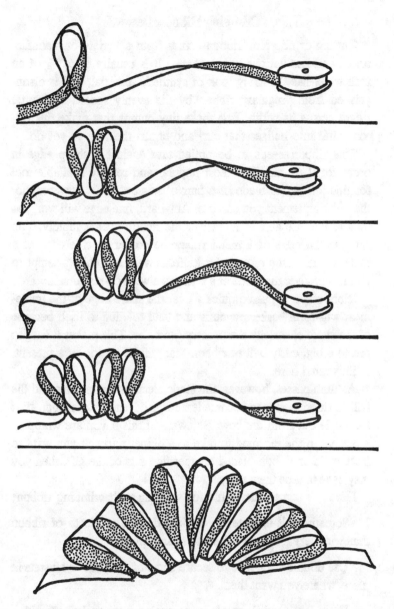

This bow is easily made from cloth ribbon (and a little glue or tape to hold the loops together).

Crimping Ribbon Bows

Curling or crimping ribbon comes from a variety of manufacturers and has various brand names. It is usually ¼ to ⅜ of an inch wide, has the shiny look of synthetic material, and is distinguished from "regular" ribbon by the evenly spaced horizontal ridges across its width. It is those tiny bumps that make this ribbon spiral into helixes that curl and unfurl the way yo-yos do.

This ribbon needs to be pulled taut against a sharp edge in order for it to curl. The most popular and readily available tool for this job is one blade of a pair of scissors. It is, however, not the only implement you can use. Any hard, fine edge will work, as long as you are able to maneuver the ribbon over it rapidly. You can use the edge of a metal ruler, the corner or side edge of a table, or the blade of a butter knife. Never let a child attempt to curl ribbon over the blade of a scissors; always do it yourself.

Ribbon that is passed quickly over the sharp edge of the implement will form corkscrew curls and tend to cling to itself because of the static electricity the process generates. This makes it easy to create a big, curly ball of ribbon that will sit on top of a present, as illustrated here.

As time passes, however, the static electricity dissipates and the ball of ribbon tends to become less formed; tendrils of ribbon start to dangle out from the bow. Be aware of this if you are wrapping a present in the morning to take to a dinner party. If you want to have curls of ribbon placed on specific parts of the gift, then you may have to tape them there.

Here are some other hints for working with crimping ribbon:

• Sometimes it is better to work with smaller pieces of ribbon than with very long ones—the latter can droop.

• Use double-stick tape to secure some of the ends or clusters in place, where you want them.

• Form long tendrils carefully, arranging them as desired, with a dab of glue or double-stick tape to hold the end of each in place.

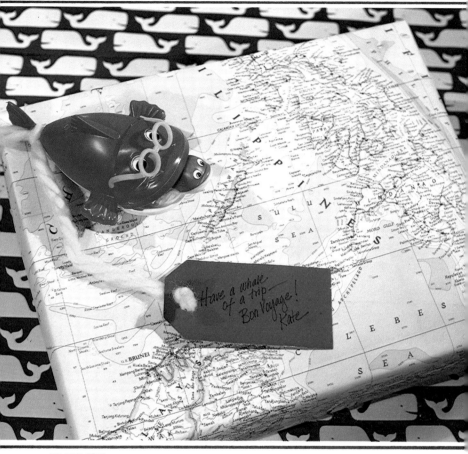

COLOR PLATE 14

Bon voyage to the traveler! Have a whale of a trip! This going-away present, with a map used in place of wrapping paper, could contain a survival kit of miniature sundries and trinkets for the lucky recipient.

COLOR PLATE 15

On the left is an example of a Torpedo Package, as described in Chapter Four. It is ideal for all types of odd-shaped gifts that don't come with boxes. The two Patchwork Packages are simple to do; their instructions are given in Chapter Two.

COLOR PLATE 16

Three distinctive bows, described in Chapter Five (top to bottom): Starburst, Pinwheel, and Looped Bows.

COLOR PLATE 17

How festive-looking these simple shopping bags can look with just a little tissue paper, a few stickers, and a ribbon! In the center of the picture, the plastic bag could even hold a cumbersome gift like a world globe, surrounded with tissue paper. The doilies and tissue paper used in these wrappings show the care you've taken, and these would all be lovely wrappings for Valentine's Day.

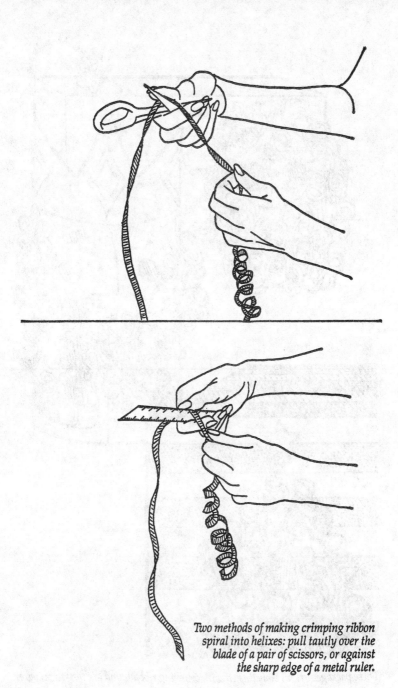

Two methods of making crimping ribbon spiral into helixes: pull tautly over the blade of a pair of scissors, or against the sharp edge of a metal ruler.

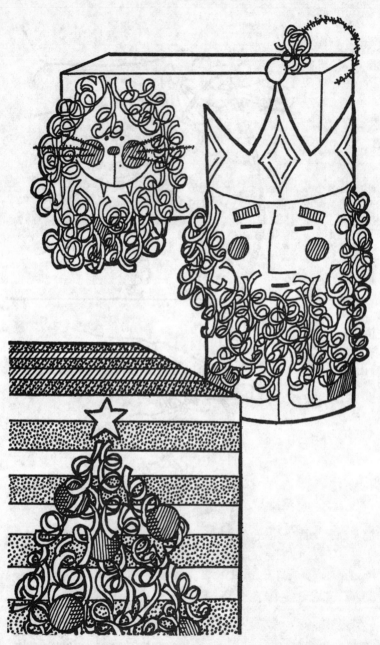

These packages are all embellished with crimping ribbon, and are easy to prepare.

This simply wrapped package is decorated with a flourish of crimping ribbon for a bow.

Following are different occasions when decorating with crimping ribbon will add that special touch to your gift:

• For a child's Communion, wrap your present (preferably held in a box with a rectangular shape) in white or silver paper. Run two wide strips of double-stick tape across the top of the box in the shape of a cross. Cover the cross shape with silver or white curled ribbon, and you have created not a bow but a beautiful, appropriate decoration.

• At Christmastime, create the same kind of effect as just mentioned—but in the shape of a tree. Imagine a box wrapped in bright red paper, with a three-dimensional evergreen tree, made from sweeping ringlet curls of green curling ribbon. In this case, because the tree is so much larger than a simple bow area or a geometric cross, your choice of adhesive for the ribbon should be something other than double-stick tape. One easy way to get the triangular shape on the gift wrap paper is to "paint" it on with rubber cement. After the tree shape is created with the glue, then attach the strands of curling ribbon.

• Curling ribbon is ideal for making hair—a lion's mane, Abraham Lincoln or Santa Claus beards, a head for a scarecrow, etc.

• This kind of ribbon is also well suited to making grass for a garden (along the bottom edge of a package, with flowers sprouting out of the lawn); fluffy, dreamy white clouds in the sky; waves in the ocean; snow underfoot; etc. (*See Flower Box in Color Plate 7.*)

• A pair of traditional wedding bells, formed from silver crimping ribbon—perhaps on glossy white paper—would make a nice package decoration for a gift earmarked for the bride and groom.

USING SCRAPS OF RIBBON

There are many types of bows that you can make with leftovers or small bits of ribbon—bows that don't look as if they have been made from scraps. They will look planned (which they are), not haphazard. The look of any bow made from scraps will vary, since the materials are less controlled. Even if the same simple technique was used to make two bows, they could look entirely different, based on the types of ribbons used, the colors present in the bows, and the lengths of the ribbon scraps.

Many of the types of bows that can be made from scraps resemble flowers. The bows seem to emerge from a central core; and although the "flowers" are not necessarily classified in a botanical encyclopedia, the suggestion of a flower with long petals, like a poinsettia, still remains.

"Scrap" Flower Bow

This type of bow is most easily made from synthetic gift wrapping ribbons and requires that each scrap piece of ribbon be *at least* 3 inches long. (It is preferable to have longer scraps—from 4 to 7 inches.) This type of flower bow can be placed anywhere on a package, which does not have to be enveloped in a horizontal and vertical ribbon configuration (as seen in the section "Tying Ribbon around a Package"). You do not need such a ribbon around the package to anchor this bow.

While it is possible to make this type of bow from cloth ribbons (with a woven edge, used for home sewing), the results will be less than satisfying. The self-sticking gift wrapping ribbons are preferable because the center of each ribbon must be twisted and secured—which is easily accomplished by moistening such ribbons. With cloth ribbons you'd have to use some type of glue and wait for it to dry. (The "Scrap" Flower Bow with Spidery Edges, however, works better with cloth ribbons, so save them for use there.)

1. Arrange scraps of ribbon by size and color. Decide what color(s) you want the "petals" of the flower to be and set aside all other ribbons. Be certain that you have at least four or five pieces of ribbon that are 3 inches minimum. If you have more, you may opt to work with four pieces of ribbon 6 inches long, three pieces of ribbon 4 inches long, etc.; the more ribbons worked into the flower, the fuller the bloom will be.

2. Trim the ends of each ribbon so that they are somewhat rounded or pointed, as desired.

3. Starting with the longest ribbons, determine the center of each piece. At that center point, moisten the ribbon and twist it so that half of it is wrong side up. (This is another good reason to use synthetic ribbons for this type of flower, since both sides of the ribbon are visible.) Make the twist tight and moisten it again so that the ribbon sticks to itself and holds that shape. You've created a whole petal. Set that piece of ribbon aside. Continue this process with all the ribbons; keep them arranged in piles according to length.

4. To make the flower shape, start with the longest pieces of ribbon; lay one on top of another so that their centers touch, but their petals fan outward in different directions. Moisten each piece of ribbon at its center so that it adheres to the one below it. If you have only four or five pieces of ribbon, each 3 inches long, then that is your entire flower. However, if you have graduated lengths of ribbons, then that is only the first layer—the bottom layer of petals on the flower.

5. Take the next batch of ribbon scraps, which are the next longest in length, and arrange them on top of the first layer. Crisscross them in the same fashion, trying to arrange them so that the ribbon petals fall in between the petals of the under layer. When the arrangement is to your taste, moisten each piece to secure it in place. If that is the end of your ribbon supply, then you are done. If you have more pieces of ribbon—even shorter—to form more petals, then attach them as described above.

6. A center for the flower is optional. If you have a piece of yellow ribbon, make a small circle; if no yellow ribbon is available, then use another color or substitute another item—

a bit of gift wrapping paper, a stray button, a tiny pompon or fringe ball, a bit of lace, a scrap of fabric, or plain construction paper.

Use 4- to 7-inch scraps of ribbon to produce this pretty flower bow.

"Scrap" Flower Bow with Spidery Edges

This is a very simple variation of the previously described "Scrap" Flower Bow, and produces an entirely different look when it is finished. To make a really full flower, you will need 1 yard of ribbon.

1. Arrange the ribbon lengths by size, using nothing smaller than a 3-inch piece. You will need at least four pieces of ribbon to make this bow. If you are working with the wider of the gift wrapping ribbons (approximately 1¼ inches wide), even with four pieces you'll get a full flower; if you are working with the narrower of the gift wrapping ribbons (approximately ¾ inch wide), four pieces will make a slightly anemic flower.

2. Without shaping the ends to be round or pointed, create the twist in the center of each piece of ribbon, as you did in Step #3 on page 132.

3. Create the flower shape as instructed previously in Step #4; and if you have graduated lengths of ribbon, follow Step #5 on page 132, as well.

4. Once the flower shape is together, you will work with one petal at a time to create its spidery edges. If you are using synthetic, self-sticking gift wrapping ribbon, use your fingers to split it apart into slivers. These ribbons will tear apart neatly and evenly with just a little tug at their edge. If you are using any other type of ribbon (including cloth), you will need a pair of scissors. Regardless of which method you use, do not cut all the way into the center. Stop at least ½ inch from the core of the ribbon twists at the flower's center. The minute you start separating the ribbon into narrower strips, you will notice that the split-apart ribbons start to splay out, creating a full flower.

5. As with the "Scrap" Flower Bow, a center for the flower is optional.

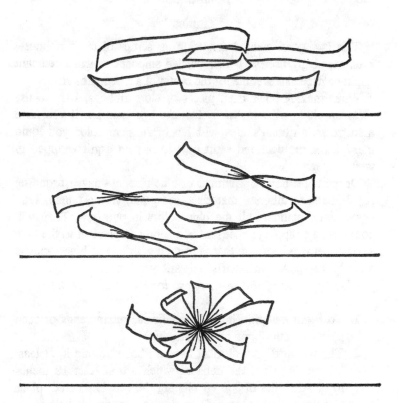

This pretty flower bow is made from scraps of gift wrapping ribbon. The ends of the ribbon have been split apart to create a full flower.

Zinnias

This is a good method for using up scraps of cloth ribbons—even seemingly useless 1-inch raveled snippets. A small remnant might be needed sometime for the center of a ribbon flower.

When making bows from pieces of cloth ribbons, I try to use them up either by color or by texture. For example, if you have assorted satin ribbon scraps, with few of the same color, you could make a big multicolored satin bow to use on a gift wrapped in white paper.

Or, perhaps, having a number of blue ribbons—navy, turquoise, royal—made of different materials—grosgrain, velvet, taffeta, satin—you could combine all the blue colors in one bow. Then you could use a wrapping paper that is a good complement to the blue (green, perhaps), or one that is printed with lots of blues—maybe a marbleized paper with swirls in a variety of blues.

(*For examples of this bow, see Color Plates 13 and 3.*)

1. To begin making Zinnia flower bows, cut the ends of each piece of cloth ribbon on the diagonal.
2. The wrapped present must have a ribbon around it, at least in one direction, the ends of which are at least 10 inches long. After the ribbon enveloping the box is secured, place these two 10-inch tails down flat on the top of the box, in opposite quadrants.
3. Starting with the largest pieces of the scrap ribbon, lay them across the secured knot on top of the package. Be careful to center each piece of ribbon on the knot and vary the placement of the ribbons as you work, crisscrossing them over each other. In this fashion, you will be forming the petals of the flower shape. However, do not place all the ribbons on the package at this point; only work with about four or five at one time.
4. When you have placed four or five lengths of ribbon on the package, carefully bring up the two 10-inch ties and make a tight overhand knot with them. This will gather up the ribbon scraps at the center and splay them out around the edges.

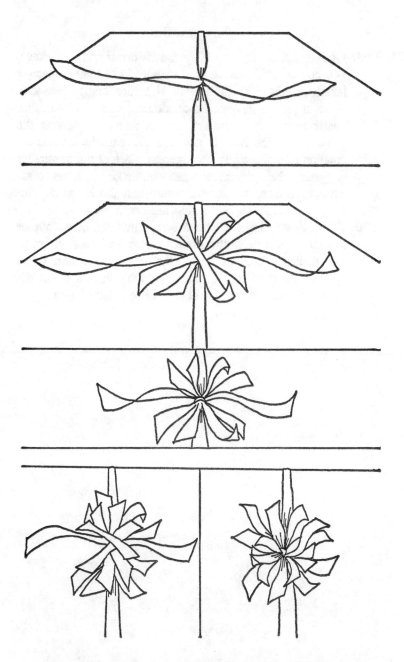

This eye-catching Zinnia bow is especially attractive when you use remnants of multicolored cloth ribbons.

5. Once again, set the two 10-inch ends down on the package. (Of course, after having used up a little of their respective lengths, neither will still be quite 10 inches long.) Place each piece of ribbon in opposite quadrants, using the two other quadrants that you did not use in Step #1. Varying the placement of the two 10-inch ends prevents the inadvertent creation of a "hole" on two opposite sides of the flower. By staggering their placement when you make the knots to secure the ribbon scraps, you ensure that the entire circumference of the flower bow will be filled with petals.

6. Continue working the ribbon scraps into the bow, four or five pieces at a time, always going from the largest pieces to the smallest, which will be on the top of the flower. When the last layer is secured, make a double knot and cut the ends of the ties so that they fit into the rest of the flower.

CHAPTER
SIX

Package Embellishments

$\mathcal{W}$henever I am out shopping I invariably buy some little trinket or novelty item that I just know is going to come in handy one day. In addition, I save everything from tiny aluminum pie plates and bright-colored plastic paperclips, to glass phials that once contained vanilla beans, corks from wine bottles, old Valentine cards, and funny Halloween facial disguises.

Even if you are not a "pack rat," collecting and saving all kinds of objects, it is still likely that you have unusual items around your home that can be utilized for novel gift wrapping. What kinds of items are there tucked away in the linen closet? What about your plastic swizzle sticks? Might you use those obsolete metal curtain rings for some novelty gift?

In stationery and novelty stores and notions departments you'll find a variety of glittery seals and stickers: from realistic animals to fanciful creatures; stars, moons, and rainbows; seasonal and holiday memorabilia, like bunnies, pumpkins, hearts, shamrocks, autumn leaves; funny pink elephants, dancing bears, ruby red "hot lips," and endless other unusual motifs.

Also look for honeycomb decorations. These paper decorations are flat when folded but when opened up fan out into three-dimensional objects. (*See Color Plate 13.*) When the two cardboard ends are opened and brought together (a complete circle), the seemingly ordinary tissue paper comes to life to make an enchanting decoration. You'll find large Santa Claus centerpieces, tiny snowmen, turkeys with ruffles of honeycomb feathers, to name a few types. Every year there are new varieties of these decorations for every holiday. I always save several of them for wrapping special gifts.

In party-goods stores you should find doilies of all types, cut-out cardboard decorations, pretty colored streamers and confetti, in addition to such novelty items as jingle bells, feathers, unusual buttons, and artificial flowers, which can provide you with lots of inspiration for a distinctive package wrap design.

*Honeycomb decorations are one of my favorite embellishments for **a** gift; they make any package a special one.*

DECORATIONS TO MAKE

One of the easiest types of decorations you can make, which require *no* special supplies (in fact, it uses up old scraps of paper), is Folded Fans. Just as assorted papers and cardboards provided the backbone for making boxes (as shown in Chapter Four), here too, papers will come in very handy. You will be able to make many beautiful embellishments with just a few folded papers.

(Right) Folded fans of all sizes can be used in endless configurations to form charming, inexpensive decorations. (Notice the "bicycle" on one package, with the wheels made from folded fans.) Save even the tiniest scraps of gift wrapping paper to make these fans.

Folded Fans

To construct a Folded Fan, all you need are gift wrapping paper, scissors, and adhesive tape.

1. For your first attempt to make this decoration, use guidelines that you pencil in along the length of the strip of paper (which is 8 inches wide and 20 inches long). Draw lines along the wrong side of the paper at 1-inch intervals. Plan on having 19 lines when you are finished.
2. Starting at one end of the paper, right side up, start folding the paper at each 1-inch mark. Make the first fold a mountain fold, and the second, a valley fold. Continue alternating folds in this manner. Be certain that the creases are sharp and crisp. When you reach the other end of the paper, you should end with a mountain fold.
3. Splay the folded piece of paper out into a fan shape, so that the first and last folds form a straight line.
4. Run a small piece of tape on the underside of the first and last folds, to join them firmly along a bottom straight line.
5. Turn the fan over, and on the wrong side of the paper, run a piece of tape, about 2 inches long, across the bottom center of the fan, catching all the folds to keep them in place.

(Right) This folded paper fan is merely a series of mountain and valley folds, with the finished piece looking very sharp, and having no sloppy edges.

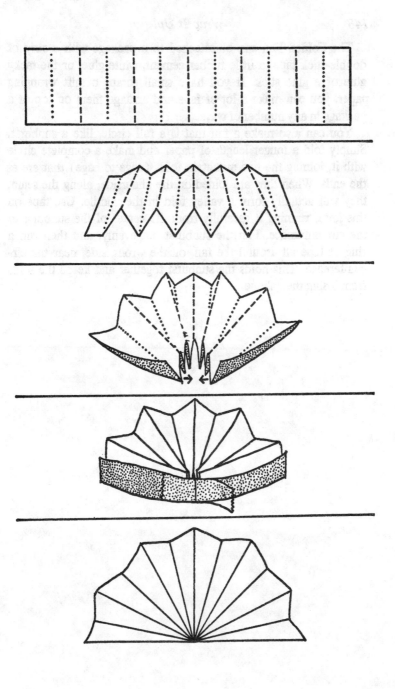

The Folded Fan can be attached to a package with a strip of double-stick tape, a little rubber cement, white glue, or the tacky glue of a glue stick. If you have small scraps of gift wrapping paper, you can make a lot of fans and arrange them on top of a package in any number of ways.

You can also make a fan that is a full circle, like a sunburst. Simply fold a longer length of paper and make a complete circle with it, joining the two mountain folds (edge to edge) that are at the ends. When they are joined on the underside, along the seam, they will actually form a valley fold in the middle. Use tape on this joint, running it carefully from the center of the sunburst to the circumference. Fan the sunburst out evenly, and then run a ring of tape all around the fan, on the wrong side, near the circumference. This holds the sunburst together and keeps the folds from losing their shape.

Ribbon Roses

The method for making Ribbon Roses presented here works with any type of cloth ribbon, preferably one without right and wrong sides. This is because both sides of the ribbon will show when you are finished. Single-faced satin ribbon has a right (shiny) and a wrong (dull) side, but they look so similar when the rose is made that it won't matter. However, on an embroidered ribbon, the wrong side is often covered with floating threads and is not very attractive. Printed ribbons are also a problem. Stick with grosgrain, moiré, velvet, or taffeta ribbons. (*See examples in Color Plates 11 and 12.*) These ribbon roses make perfect decorations for wedding gifts.

The amount of ribbon you need for each flower will be dependent on how large and full a rose you want, as well as the width of the ribbon. For a medium-sized rose you will need approximately 1 yard of ribbon, width #9. The finished rose will require only 2 feet of ribbon, but until you learn how to make this rose from yardage feeding directly off the spool, it will be easier to cut the 1 yard piece and work with it unencumbered.

You will also need a small piece of wire, a pipe cleaner, or plastic bag twist-tie to fasten the ribbon when it is made. (You could also sew the ends of the ribbon together, although it would take a bit more time.)

1. Working on a flat surface with the wrong side of the ribbon facing toward you, fold the ribbon in half to determine the halfway (18-inch) point, along the length. Mark it. Open it up so that it is flat on the table again.
2. At the halfway point, make a 45-degree angle fold, so that the right side of the ribbon on that half (labeled "x") is facing you after you make that fold (*Fig. 1*).
3. Fold the other half of the ribbon (labeled "y") over "x," following the edge of "x." This fold brings "y" back over the other half ("x"). The two halves of the ribbon are now at right angles to each other, and each is face up (*Fig. 2*).
4. Working with "x," fold it along the edge of and over "y," so that the wrong side of "x" is face up. The two halves of the ribbon still form right angles to each other, but are in different relative positions (*Fig. 3*).
5. Return to "y," which is face up, and fold it over "x," so that it is wrong side up. The two halves of the ribbons are still at right angles to each other, but are once again in different relative positions (*Fig. 4*). The small triangular shape you created in Step #1 will be below this pile of folds.
6. Continue this folding process (*Figs. 5 and 6*) to complete the cycle. (Note that Figs. 2 and 5 are the same.) Repeat this process until one or both ribbon halves are exhausted.
7. When both lengths of the ribbon are exhausted and you cannot make any more folds, hold both ends of the ribbon together and allow the small pile of folds to spring open. Hold the ribbon chain so that it hangs down toward the floor; use one hand to hold both ends of the ribbon (*Fig. 7*). With your free hand, start to pull on one end of the ribbon (*Fig. 8*), forcing the chain of the ribbon to squash up on the other side of your hand. Continue to pull at least 10 inches of the ribbon through. As you do this, turn your hand over so that you can observe the formation of the rose. When you have a rose shape that you like, stop pulling the end of the ribbon.
8. Arrange the petals of the rose so that they fall on alternating sides. Using wire, fasten the underside of the flower securely (or stitch it in place). Cut the excess ribbon from the underside, leaving enough to tie the rose to the package (or use a twist-tie to attach the rose to the ribbon on the box).

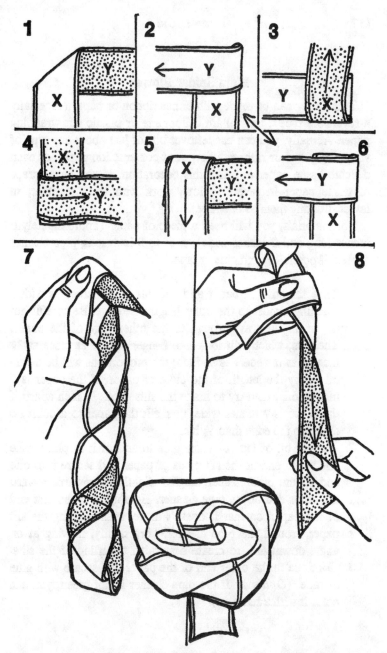

How to make ribbon roses (note that the right side of the ribbon is the shaded side): The steps are simple and repeat themselves quickly. Notice that Fig. 2 and Fig. 6 have the same configuration. After you get to Fig. 6 in the instructions, repeat the steps starting with Fig. 2, until the length of ribbon is exhausted.

Plain Spider Flower

This flower can be made with either ribbon or paper (especially a reversible type); or a pliant cellophane or plastic gift wrapping paper. Actually, you can use leftover bits of just about any type of wrapping paper or ribbon, all types of construction paper, or even delicate tissue paper to make this decoration. If you have scraps of tissue paper in several colors, work with them together, in layers, treating them as one sheet.

For materials, you will need a piece of paper (approximately 6 inches long and 2 inches wide), a 6- to 9-inch long pipe cleaner (green, if possible), and glue or tape.

1. Take the strip of paper and cut slits in it, across its width, reaching almost to the other lengthwise edge. Be careful not to cut all the way through to the other edge of the paper. The slits, which will look like fringe, can be as close as ⅛ inch or as far apart as ½ inch; the proportions will be determined by the length of the piece of paper. If the paper is 6 inches long, then try to make the slits about ¼ inch apart; if the paper is 2 inches wide, then slit the paper to a point no closer to the edge than ½ inch.

2. Using a bit of tape or some glue to anchor it in place, take one width end of the slit piece of paper and secure it to one end of the pipe cleaner, angled slightly downward, toward the other end of the pipe cleaner. Holding onto the first end of the paper, so that it doesn't move, start winding the slit paper around the pipe cleaner, very tightly, moving at an angle downward, to create a spiraled unfurling of the slits.

3. Continue to the other end of the paper and secure with glue or tape. (*Optional:* If the pipe cleaner is not green, you can color it with a felt pen.)

This flower can be used individually along with a gift card; or used in a bouquet of flowers on top of the package; or wound up with a ribbon and added to the bow on the package. A small bouquet of these spidery flowers makes a pretty presentation in summery colors on pastel paper or in gem tones on a bright solid color, particularly if they are made with layers of tissue.

The more you angle the spiral around the central core, the longer the flower will be; if you really want a long and curly-looking plant, use paper that is at least 4 to 5 inches wide and make long, narrowly spaced slits in it, so that when the fringe cascades down the sides of the stem (or trunk, in this case), it will look like the leaves of a tropical royal palm tree.

Spidery Mum

This flower is made quite similarly to the Plain Spider Flower (see above section for materials to use, and accompanying illustration). It also works well with pliant material—the softer, the better. For a full, just about life-sized flower, you will need paper about 4 to 5 inches wide and about 8 to 9 inches long, with at least four layers of paper stacked on top of each other. (*See Color Plate 9.*)

1. Stack the papers, ribbons, or cloth scraps on top of each other, so that the lengthwise edges are not aligned, but rather tiered, allowing each layer to show about ¼ to ½ inch at the edge. (Width edges remain flush.)
2. Slit along the lengthwise edge, at which the bottommost layer shows. Make the slits quite narrow; they should nearly reach the other lengthwise edge, but not cut all the way through to it on any layer.
3. Holding the layers of paper so that the bottommost layer will be on the inside, start to roll the papers along the width, holding the bottom edges tightly. This roll will not be angled, but rather will progress in a straight line, so that all the layers of paper stay in the same position relative to each other. As you roll the paper you will notice that the abundant slits start to blossom out as a spider mum. If you have used a great deal of paper, then the effect will look more like a regular mum.
4. To fasten the end, secure it with glue or tape; or remove the pipe cleaner and use a stapler to secure the bottom of the flower. This would be a suitable method for fastening the flower when you know that the bottom part won't show and you don't want a stem (for example, when you are going to put the flower in the middle of a package and surround it with construction paper leaves, fanning out to the edges of the box).

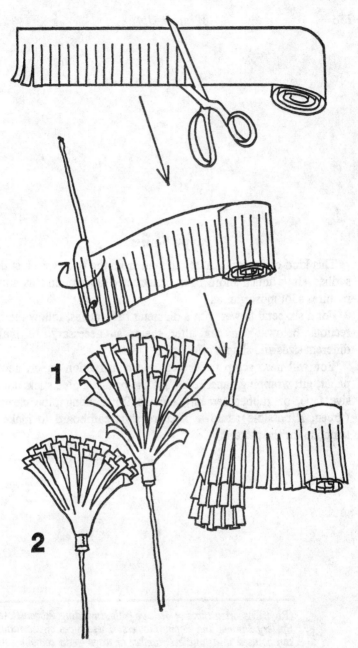

A Plain Spider Flower (Fig. 1) and a Spidery Mum (Fig. 2) are made basically in the same manner. The only difference is the way the papers are wrapped around the pipe cleaners.

Poppy Flower

This kind of flower is quite different from the two types just described. It is much more of a constructed flower, and as such, requires a lot more gluing.

For a six-petal flower with a diameter of 4 inches, follow the directions below. You can alter them, as necessary, to make different sizes and shapes of poppies.

You will need scrap paper (colored construction paper, newspaper, gift wrapping paper, etc.) for the petals; a glue stick, adhesive tape, or rubber cement; a 6- to 9-inch long pipe cleaner (green, if possible); and a piece of shirt cardboard to make a template for the pattern.

(Right) Assorted types of package frills, including Ribbon Roses, Spidery Mums, and Poppy Flowers. These types of decorations can be used in a limitless number of ways — in combinations, singly, on the top or sides of boxes, made from diverse papers, etc.

1. Cut out a replica of the petal pattern, shown here, from the shirt cardboard. Use it as a guide and trace it onto the paper or fabric that you will use for the petals, twelve times to make six petals. (Always cut out double the number of desired petals.)

2. Attach a pipe cleaner to the wrong side of one petal, securing it with glue or tape.

3. Coat the wrong side of a second petal with glue and attach this petal to the first one so that the two are aligned perfectly around the edges. Be sure that the wrong sides are together, so that the right side of the paper appears on the outside of each one.

4. Repeat the above procedure with the other ten petals, so that when you are finished, you have six two-sided petals.

5. Gather all six petals in a circle; curl them, using the pipe cleaners inserted in each as a means to shape the petals into a flower formation. You will be able to make a number of shapes with the wired petals: outwardly turned petals, with their tips turned inward; tuliplike blossoms, with the petals extending upward; shooting-fountain-style petals, that seem to simply gush up from their stems.

6. As you work, twine the six pipe cleaners together, to keep the stem secure and keep the petals bound. If desired, you can add leaves that are anchored into the twists of the pipe-cleaner stems.

7. When the petals and stems are finished, add a center to the flower, using a piece of paper, a bit of cloth, glitter, a pompon, or other type of trim—even a large gold sequin.

Remember, no matter what type(s) of flowers you make, you can use a large one alone as the center of a package's decoration; a small one alone, as a delicate, understated adornment; a cluster or bouquet, for emphasis, to mimic the wrapping paper. Do whatever suits the package, the paper, the recipient, and the message or mood you want to convey.

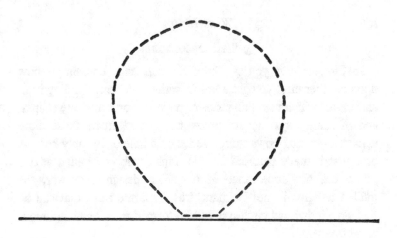

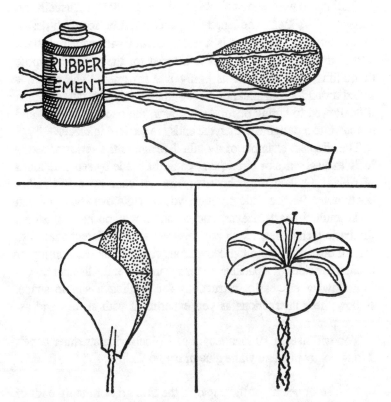

The pattern of this Poppy Flower can easily be enlarged or decreased to accommodate whatever size or shape flower you wish to make.

Quilled Decorations

In Chapter Five you saw how you can stack one simple bow upon another until you get a larger, rather full bow. Quilling is an ancient art which uses thin strips of paper to form intricate shapes, and in some ways the principles that helped create those more elaborate-looking bows from a series of simple ones apply here. A bow that is made from concentric rings of ribbon, joined at one point, has the appearance of a quilled design. However, the quilled design will not be made from separate rings that can be traced to individual circles; it will be formed from one continuous ring of paper.

Quilling requires narrow strips of paper that are usually no wider than ¼ inch. The length of paper required for each design varies, but 8 to 10 inches is a good amount with which to start. Although there are papers manufactured for the specific purpose of quilling, you can just as easily use streamers. The paper is rolled around a thin stick, or more suitably, a bobby pin, and then it is allowed to spring open. As it opens, the paper is pushed and shaped into a design and then the ends are secured in place.

The simplest example of a quilled design is the series of seemingly endless rings or circles that could be made by separate loops of ribbon. Quilled rings, however, are not concentric, but rather continuous. With a little practice, you will discover that you can make quilled hearts, leaves, and so on. Once you have mastered the basic techniques, try to put together a few different shapes to form a design. The quilled decorations can then be used on top or around the sides of a package to form a unique embellishment.

Following are basic instructions for quilling a simple shape. Follow these instructions as you experiment with shapes and assorted papers.

You will need a 10-inch length of ¼-inch-wide streamer paper, a long bobby pin, and white glue or a glue stick.

1. Insert one end of the paper in the firm grip of the tip ends of a bobby pin, so that the paper is secure and will not pop out.

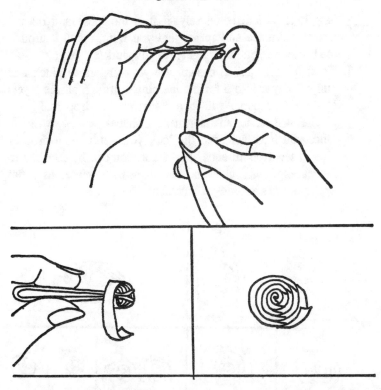

2. Working with the inherent curve in the paper, start rolling the paper around the ends of the bobby pin in a continuous action. Pull gently, but not so hard as to dislodge the assembly—just enough to keep the wrappings from getting too much slack in them.

3. When you have reached the end of the streamer, gently push the entire coiled paper off the bobby pin. If it doesn't move easily, don't force it. Release the loose end a little bit to allow more slack to go back into the rolled streamer. As you remove the coil from the bobby pin, hold it securely in the other hand, so that it doesn't jump out and unravel.

4. When the paper is off the bobby pin, place it on a table and allow it to spring open, just a little bit at first; then, slowly, a little more. Watch the shape as it forms. If it is too tight,

help it to widen; conversely, if it is too loose and doesn't have the bounce and spring that you want, recoil it around the bobby pin, pulling it tighter as you work.

5. To shape the quilled design, use your fingers to pinch and pull the paper into a form. One pinch through all the layers of the coiled paper will give a sort of tear-drop look; two pinches will render an assortment of shapes.

6. Once you have achieved the look you want, use a drop of glue to secure both ends. The decoration can be attached to the package with glue and can be worked either as a flat appliqué or as a stand-up ornament.

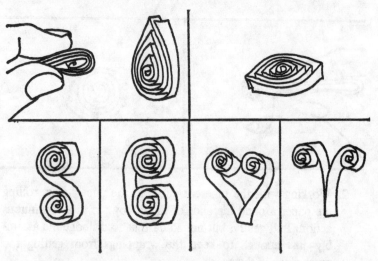

Quilled decorations provide you with interesting shapes which can be used on the top of a package in diverse arrangements.

OTHER PACKAGE EMBELLISHMENTS

Many types of decorations for the tops of your packages have been discussed in this and previous chapters. Hopefully the ideas presented here will spark your creative energies. Then, perhaps sometime in the future, if you see a pretty shell on the beach, for example, you'll realize that if you collect several of them you can decorate a package with a beach motif, or perhaps even use one spectacular shell as a single decoration and write the recipient's name on it.

Seals, Tags, and Labels

Don't confine yourself to the traditional seals, tags, and labels that are sold in most stores. Although they may be lovely, you can assuredly come up with other ideas that will be much more novel.

• Spell out the recipient's name on the top of a box using old buttons, which probably abound in your sewing kit. Write the name first with pencil, very lightly, and go over those marks with a line of glue, and then attach the buttons. Or, attach each button separately, by putting a dab of glue on the back. Of course, the type of adhesive you use (white glue, glue stick, or double-stick tape) will vary depending on the wrapping of the package.

• Spell out the message you wish to convey using slivers of paper—but not just any kind of paper. Use a paper you probably have never thought of using—for instance, paint chip samples from the nearby hardware store. Just about every paint chip is actually a strip with six or seven colors on it. Cut them up and cut each in half lengthwise, so that you have long, thin strips of paper. Glue them onto the top of a package, to spell out whatever you want to. Needless to say, this would look better on a solid background wrapping paper and it would be absolutely marvelous on black or white paper.

• You can use pipe cleaners to spell out a word or words. If the package is large, you can use the pipe cleaners in their full length. If the pipe cleaners are too big for the box, cut them up into smaller 2-inch pieces, for example, and make block letters to form whatever you want to say.

• If you have an old Scrabble® set (or any type of letter-oriented game), use those tiles to make words on the top of the package.

• Alphabet letters from alphabet soup can be dried and pasted on a package.

• Cut-outs from newspapers and magazines can be used to convey a special message or a clue-type hint as to what's inside the gift.

• Stationery stores and art supply shops have beautifully designed letters that can either be pressed or rubbed onto a package; and they are not as expensive as the type a professional artist uses. There are other types of letters that are not rubbed on, but are pulled from their backings and then placed on the package.

• For the bride and groom, try a little rice. First, use a glue stick to write the message on the package and then sprinkle rice all over it. It will adhere only where the glue is.

The above trick can also be used for decorating kitchen or food-related gifts, by using beans, breakfast cereals, etc. For best results, use a solid-colored paper or a small print that is not too busy, so that the message can be read.

• For the handyman, try the same idea, using sawdust for the lettering over the glue.

• Another variation on the above theme is to use other novelty items that you find around the house, that you wouldn't necessarily associate with gift wrapping—paper clips, for instance. If you look around stationery stores, you'll notice that paper clips come in a vast array of sizes, shapes, and colors. Use a variety of shapes and sizes to add more interest to the lettering, although the traditional shaped paper clip will also look fine. Use white glue sparingly (remember, it will dry clear) to spell out initially on the package the word or words. Then place the paper clips on the glue line and allow to dry. This would be an apt way to present a gift to a new office worker, a retiring one, or a friend who just landed a new job.

• A gift tag can be made from a common shipping label. Even the plainest ones with ruled and lined spaces for the address can be decorated, or cut into an interesting shape. The large manila tags with string ties can easily be decorated with stamps, seals, or colored markers, to look a little more festive. Rubber stamps are especially popular these days and you may come across all kinds of unlikely images, including flying fish, puckered lips, or even hamburgers. Ink a row of a particular motif around the edges of a manila shipping tag and you have a good gift tag. The same is true of all other types of shipping labels or commercial packaging labels.

• An inexpensive way to make a gift tag is to make use of the greeting cards you get at holiday time. Go through the cards and cut out some of the larger motifs from them—a large bouquet of red roses, hearts, lace, and flowers (from a Valentine's Day card, for example), or a shiny Irish shamrock, or a smiling pumpkin. These cut-outs will make good gift tags, once you punch a hole in them, near one edge of the design. You can use a simple hole puncher from the stationery store for a clean-edged, round hole through which you can insert a ribbon, to make the tag hang. Usually, the other side of the design will be white, since most greeting cards are constructed in a way that results in plain, undecorated paper on the interior folded sections.

• You can use the types of tags that are sold as key rings and key identifiers in your gift decorations. These are generally small, round, white heavy-stock paper, encircled by a small metal band. They have string or metal loops to which keys can be attached. Remove the metal or string and replace it with a pretty ribbon, bright yarn, or novelty fiber. The white label can also be decorated with a large gold star, a seal, a tiny novelty item, or covered with a checker, poker chip, etc.—whatever might be appropriate for the recipient. Use the other side for writing the recipient's name, and if there is room, a short message.

• Some cards from an old deck could be used as gift tags *if* there is room on either side for a message. Punch a hole near one corner of the card to insert a ribbon or string for it to hang.

• Seals of all types are relatively inexpensive and can be used in myriad ways to decorate a package. They can be worked all around the perimeter of a box, or in a design on top of it. They can be used to make a large initial in the middle of the package, or they can make a squiggly design over the top. One large, highly decorative seal can be used alone, right in the center of the top, to make an easily decorated package.

Cut-outs, Appliqués, Stencils, and Doilies

The types of items you can use as cut-outs from greeting cards are often prepackaged from paper goods manufacturers; regardless of the source, they can be put to use on top of a package as an appliqué, either glued or adhered with double-stick tape. You can use almost anything as an appliqué on a package.

Also, keep in mind that you don't have to confine your decorations to the top of a box. For example, a pretty floral motif on the top of a package made with several paper or cloth roses could be echoed on each of the four sides of the package with small, single roses. Likewise, a cut-out on top of the box could be complemented with other similar motifs around the sides. There are many ways you could implement this idea. Decorate the top of the box with a large doily and silhouette and then mimic the motif on the sides of the box, only in a smaller dimension. (*Color Plate 17 shows some ways to use doilies in package wrapping.*)

(Left) Using an odd assortment of "found" objects from around the house, you can decorate the tops of packages to create fantasies, abstract designs, and realistic pictures. Notice the nuts, bolts, nails, quilled papers, and spools of thread embellishing these packages.

Pretty lacy doilies can spruce up even the simplest packages, worked alone, with silhouettes on them, or in clusters with bows. Use your imagination.

Following are a few more ideas for using these types of decorations:

• Place a doily on top of a package and tack it gently to the paper with a tiny piece of double-stick tape, placed on one of the solid areas of the doily, not on one of its lacy parts. Do not press the tape down firmly. You will want to lift it up afterward without marring the paper, so do it gently. Cover the sides of the package with newspaper, to protect it. Use a contrasting-color spray paint and coat the top of the package delicately. Allow to dry thoroughly. When you remove the doily, you will have its design left—in paint, against the wrapping paper.

• Use the same idea as above, but with a slight variation—wrap the package in newspaper and use a bold contrasting color for the spray paint, like red. Don't bother masking the sides of the package, so that the red paint forms a misted, less colorful coat there. This would also look striking on a white ground, such as tissue paper.

• Select a cut-out shape that you want to silhouette, such as a leaf, and spray paint all around it. Or use regular paint, sprinkled onto the package with a toothbrush, to give a mottled look. When the paint is dry, remove the leaf or other silhouette shape, leaving its impression free from paint, and surrounded by the color in a misty, spraylike pattern.

•Stencils can provide you with another means for both lettering and designing. You can stencil a geometric motif onto a package using a pencil to lightly mark the placement of the pattern. After you have finished drawing it, use white glue to outline it and then fill it in with a thin coat of glue. After that, sprinkle glitter all over the box, and where there is glue, you will get a pattern.

• Children can use stencils easily to color in messages and designs of their choosing. Stencils come in so many varieties that you can even find one with a map of the United States, not to mention assorted floral designs, flasks and urns for science projects, and so forth.

OTHER NOVELTY ITEMS

Many of the items that I've discussed in previous sections for use in gift wrapping are novelties. There are many other types of things you can find in discount and paper goods stores that can be put to use, as well. For example, if you find plastic bags of jingle bells at Christmastime, a pretty bow could be added to a few bells to top off a package, making your gift a musical one. You could also thread the bells onto the ribbon, since jingle bells are manufactured with a self-loop at the top, made expressly for that purpose.

Party toothpicks, decorated with filaments or curlicues of bright-colored papers and cellophanes are other great novelty items for gift wrapping. You can glue them to a package top in a geometric design, starburst, or other shape. In addition, all kinds of party baskets and favors fall into the novelty area—tiny nut cups, small folding umbrellas, clusters of fruits, silky butterflies, wicker miniatures, small corrugated cardboard decorations.

In sewing or notions departments you are likely to find plastic bags filled with rhinestone studs, sequins, feathers, embroidered and printed sew-on patches, and endless types of metal fastenings. A plain belt buckle might be used to construct a "belt" around a package—especially one wrapped in a very tailored style, for a man. (*See Color Plate 1.*) The ribbon, in this case, would be wrapped around the girth of the package, and buckled right through the belt buckle. This is also an appropriate wrapping if the recipient has just lost weight.

What can you do with small, fluffy feathers? You could use them to make a bird, almost as an appliqué, on the top of the package. (*See Color Plate 10.*) Even if you don't know how to draw, improvise with two circles and two straight-lined feet. The outline can be made with white glue and the center filled in with a glue stick. The feathers could then be applied to the bird's shape. A small sequin or button could be used for an eye, and paper, pipe cleaners, or cut strips of ribbon could be used to make the feet.

Other than using feathers to make a bird decoration, you might apply your creative efforts to make flowers out of feathers, or even make a "feather garden," as if the feathers are growing out of the box. Most packages of novelty 2-inch-long feathers are inexpensive and can be used in a variety of ways on a package—as hair, grass, clouds, etc.

Glass, wooden, and plastic beads also fall into the novelty category. Wooden beads could be used to make an animal's face on a package for a small child—just use a large wooden bead for a nose, two for the eyes, and a series of beads for the mouth. You could even add a few pipe cleaners or toothpicks to make the whiskers. Beads can be used to spell out a name, make an abstract design, or a more realistic one, like a bow.

Here are some other gift wrapping ideas using novelty items:

• Spray paint a cache of bottlecaps outdoors, which are laid out on newspaper. Then decorate the top of each cap with a decal flower and attach them to the top of a package as a bouquet, on pipe cleaner or paper stems, flat against the package, as a picture, etc.

• *Empty* matchbook covers might make a good top-of-the-package decoration. They can be placed all in a row, or in a symmetric design, and would be ideal for any package that has anything to do with travel. Just use as many matchbooks as possible from out-of-town restaurants, for example, in your design.

• Foodstuffs, such as uncooked pastas, are well suited to make top-of-package designs. Macaroni, seashells, pinwheels, bows, and a panoply of noodles are all on the grocery shelf and probably in your kitchen as well. Even a dozen pieces of pasta can make a design, spell a word, or "grow" as flowers on gift packages. They can also be painted or sprayed gold—for example, to use as ornaments decorating a paper appliqué Christmas tree on top of a holiday package.

• Here's an item you probably have never thought of—eyeglass lenses. A shop selling eyeglasses will invariably have a supply of extra lenses that gets thrown out once a week or so. Go in and ask for a few. You can decorate the top of a package easily using two as the basis for eyeglasses on a funny face. This is especially good for children, whose drawings are usually not very "realistic." Use a solid-colored background paper for the wrapping and draw a circular face on top, using colored markers or crayons. Glue the two lenses in place as glasses, and draw an irregular frame around them. Add a nose and big smiling mouth, and if possible, some curly yarn or crimped ribbon hair. Draw the ears in under the mop of hair, and then add a cartoon-style balloon coming from the mouth, in which to write the message.

Be inventive with your gift decorations, and don't be afraid to experiment. Look at an object and think, "If that were the only item available to me for decorating the top of this package, how could I use it? What could I do with it? Could it be painted? Could it be decorated? Will it hold anything? Can I put things in it that will further decorate the package? Can I put items around it? Will it hold a tag? Can I write on it?" The more you force yourself to use your own resources in gift wrapping, the more distinctive and special your packages will become. And ultimately, the less money you'll spend shopping for supplies.

CHAPTER SEVEN

Special Decorated Package Designs

*N*ow that you have the tools and necessary basic information at your fingertips, it's time to move on to a few examples of special packages to wrap. These are all ideas that you can execute with items found around the home, and all can be done in a relatively short time. Some packages may require specific supplies, planning, or preparation. If that is the case, it is mentioned at the beginning of the instructions. General materials are omitted, since basic supplies for gift wrapping have been discussed in Chapter Two and elsewhere throughout this book. Only special, out-of-the-ordinary materials will be listed with each package.

Remember, these are only ideas—hopefully, they will ignite your imagination, so that you can use them in other fashions suitable to your particular packages. Use the basic instructions provided as a springboard. You will not find exact measurements for each piece of paper or ribbon, each size and shape of box, or each set of embellishments; you will find general procedural information. Try to use this so that it will be most valuable to you—to invent wrappings on your own for those hard-to-wrap problem packages or those basically uninteresting ones (such as a tie in a box which everyone knows its contents).

If you have questions about a basic technique used in the following packages, return to the general text for specific instructions.

Tie Package (Color Plate 1)

Here's a special gift wrapping for when you're faced with the problem of how to wrap that easy-to-detect tie box. Why not add a touch of humor to the wrapping and make a tie on the outside of the box?

Materials:
No special materials are needed. The type of glue will vary, depending on the paper or fabric being used. (*Note:* The package shown in Color Plate 1 was made with a self-adhesive paper.)

1. Cover the under section of the box separately from the top. Here, the top is covered with a pretty grid pattern in primary colors.
2. Draw a tie pattern on a piece of newspaper or a brown paper bag. Cut it out and trace it lightly on the top of the tie box.
3. Next, draw the stripe pattern on the tie, as shown. Cut the blocks of stripes out and use each block as a pattern to cut a piece of the selected paper or fabric that will make the design.
4. Place the cut paper or fabric on the tie box in the tie configuration. Glue each in place separately.
5. Add a "collar" made from white paper or fabric at the top center of the box.

Mitten Package (Color Plate 1)

Like the preceding package, this is one idea that you can use either to add a touch of humor to a glove wrapping, or to disguise another package that might come in a similar type of box (several pairs of men's socks, for example).

Materials:
Same as for Tie Package

1. Wrap the package normally.
2. Trace a hand shape on newspaper or a brown paper bag. Only an outline is necessary; you do not need to draw the fingers. Then, smooth out the perimeter to make a mitten shape.
3. Cut out the pattern and trace it onto a sheet of coordinating gift wrapping paper. Adhere the paper to the box, centering it.
4. Add a little piece of trim or ribbon at the "wrist" of the mitten.

Denim Pocket Package (Color Plate 1)

This package has been alluded to previously, in the section on Fabrics in Chapter Two. It's a fun wrapping and uses up a pocket of an old pair of jeans you may have stored somewhere, just waiting to be used as patches.

Materials:
Denim pocket or small piece of denim cut to pocket size
Belt buckle
Pinking shears
Small square of fabric
Piece of vinyl, leather, plastic, self-adhesive paper, etc.

1. Wrap the package normally.
2. Glue the denim pocket or denim fabric to the package, as shown, applying glue to the perimeter of the pocket only. Keep the pocket section open, so it can function as a pocket. Allow the glue to dry a bit before continuing, so that you don't dislodge the pocket from its place.
3. Wrap the "belt" around the package, with the belt buckle inserted over it. If necessary, use the point of the scissors to make a belt notch for the buckle. (*Do not allow children to do this!*) If a hole puncher is available, use that.
4. Insert a small square of fabric into the pocket, as shown, to look like a handkerchief or bandanna.

Shirt Package (Color Plate 2)

This package, like the previous two, is fun to make. It uses up scraps of ribbon and buttons you may have around the house. Use self-adhesive gift wrapping ribbons or even strips of cloth to make the "stripes" of the shirt.

Materials:
Buttons (seven are used here; they do not have to match)

1. Wrap the package normally. Here, this one is wrapped in a brown paper bag. (*Note:* If oversized packages are to be wrapped, use sheets of brown kraft paper.)
2. Using a ruler as a guide, space the ribbon or fabric stripes on the box, starting with the center and working outward toward each side of the box. Do not glue them in place; merely mark the box where the stripes should go.
3. Cut a collar shape from newspaper, as a pattern, and use it to make a collar shape from the ribbon or fabric. Adhere it to the package at the "neck."
4. Adhere the stripes to the package, tucking them under the "collar," if necessary.
5. Add "cuffs" on the sides of the package, using the same ribbon or fabric.
6. Add a "pocket" to the shirt and a "handkerchief" coming out from it.
7. Add a tie at the neck. Here, this one is made with a double bow.
8. Glue the buttons in place and allow them to dry before handling.

Cut-outs and Lettering (Color Plate 2)

This is a decorated box that couldn't be easier to prepare. Even kids should have fun making this one.

Materials:

This package can be easily done with scraps of self-adhesive paper. If you use fabric, use spray adhesive to secure the design in place. If you use construction paper, a white paste will work nicely.

1. Wrap the package normally. Here, a brown paper bag was used. (*Note:* If oversized packages are to be wrapped, use brown kraft paper.)
2. With double-stick tape, outline block letters that spell out the message you want on the package. Here, "For Dad" is emblazoned onto the package with ½-inch-wide tape.
3. Pieces of fabric should be cut to fit over the tape to spell out the message. They do not have to fit precisely; as long as they are a little bit wider than the tape, they will stick. If they are narrower, a bit of tape will show and mar the package's appearance.
4. Cut out geometric shapes from an assortment of fabrics and spray the back of each with adhesive. Apply them to the package in any configuration, as desired. They can be random (as here) or in a design.

Santa's Sleigh (Color Plate 3)

This package is certain to please even the most confirmed Scrooge at holiday time. You'll also delight children because the top has lots of tiny little packages. Some (or all) of the tiny packages can be real—filled with balloons, trinkets, etc. If you have a sleigh, like the one shown, you may want to fill the packages with miniature gifts. If you cannot locate a sleigh, you can simply make a mound of pretty packages—without any contents—that will be decorative and probably used later for other purposes.

Materials:
Sleigh (this novelty item can be found at Christmastime in discount stores, novelty or gift shops, or party stores)
Cotton balls for snow (regular sheet cotton will also work well)
Candy canes for decoration
Miniature Santa
Cardboard inner core from paper toweling
Lids from miniature jewelry boxes

1. Wrap the package normally.
2. Place a layer of cotton on top of the package, as snow, and glue it in place.
3. Glue the sleigh in place on the package. Use ribbon to make "tracks" and glue it in place.
4. To make small packages for the sleigh: Cover lids of small jewelry boxes, as if they were wrapped gifts. Cut sections of the cardboard core of paper toweling into small pieces (2 inches long) and wrap those as if they, too, were presents. Pile all the packages in the sleigh and glue them in place.
5. Add decorative touches—a miniature Santa, candy canes, a bow, etc.

Baby Bassinet (Color Plate 4)

This is the perfect gift wrapping for a baby shower. Be certain to select a pretty paper for this package, one that has a charming motif.

Materials:
Doilies
Baby bassinet (novelty item, often found in discount stores)
Styrofoam spheres, 1½ and 2 inches in diameter
Colored tissue paper
Colored pipe cleaners

1. Wrap the package normally.
2. Make a special area for the bassinet by placing several colored doilies over the wrapping paper and gluing them in place.
3. Glue the bassinet in place, with decorative ribbons around the bottom outside perimeter.
4. To make the "balloons": Cover Styrofoam balls with tissue paper, as shown, and tie the extra wrapping together with a curlicue ribbon. Make a good number of ribbon tendrils, to cascade over the package. Insert a pipe cleaner into a Styrofoam ball at the gathering.
5. Glue pipe cleaners into the bassinet and fill the bassinet (when glue is dry) with small candies.

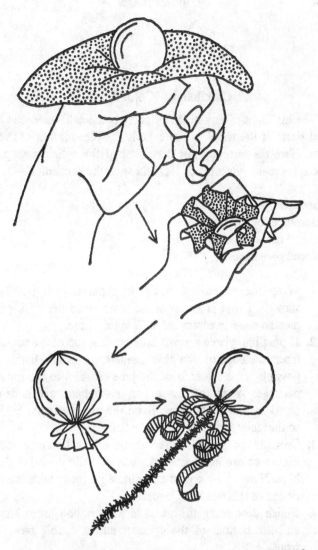

Covering Styrofoam balls with tissue paper. Insert the ball into the center of a large circle of tissue paper and gather at the end. Tie off securely.

Candlelight (Color Plate 5)

The highlight of any birthday party is the cake—and one of the best parts of the ritual of the cake is the blowing out of the candles. Here's a birthday gift treatment of the cylinder shape that takes its creative inspiration from those birthday candles.

Materials:
Colored cellophane papers
Colored tissue papers
Colored pipe cleaners

1. Wrap the cylindrical box's lid separately, if possible, as shown. If that is not possible, then wrap the package with pleated ends, as discussed in Chapter Three.
2. If possible, pierce a small hole into the top of the package to insert the ends of two pipe cleaners, as shown. If this is not possible, tape the ends of the pipe cleaners to the top of the package. After the tissue and cellophane are added, the taped ends will not show. Bend the pipe cleaners, as shown, so that they form the shape of a flame.
3. Crumple up some colored tissue and cellophane together. Flame colors are best—red, orange, yellow, and a dash of blue. Here, those colors coordinate perfectly with the candle design of this wrapping paper.
4. Finish decorating the package with ribbon around the top and the bottom of the cylinder and a double bow on the front.

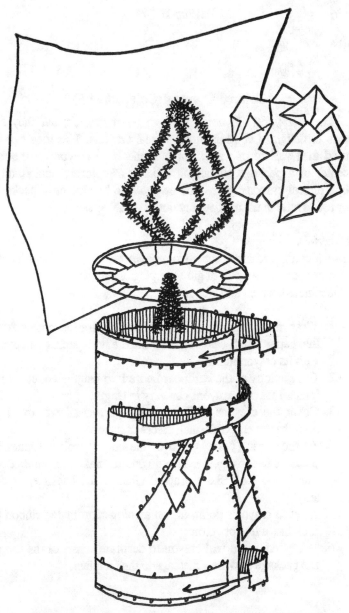

Building the flame on the candle. Use pipe cleaners as the base and insert crumpled up tissue paper and colored cellophane to represent the flame.

Colored Crayons (Color Plate 5)

These crayons will never write or color a book, but they are sure to delight a child as much as real crayons. This idea can be used in a variety of ways: put just one large crayon on the top center of a package containing a batch of coloring books and a box of real crayons; place one or two side by side on a package; or use several in a row, popping out of a package.

Materials:

2 or 3 cardboard inner cores from paper toweling, or 1 cardboard inner core from a roll of gift wrapping paper
Coordinated papers and ribbon

1. Wrap the package normally. Here, inspiration comes from the paper itself (as with the Candlelight package above), with its crayon motif.
2. Cut sections of the cardboard core into lengths about 3 to 4 inches long; the crayons can vary in length.
3. Cover the crayons with colored paper, as shown, overlapping the flat end with small pieces of paper.
4. At the other (pointy) end of the crayon, roll a triangular piece of paper together into a cone to make the point. Decorate it to look like a crayon. Glue to the package, as desired.
5. At each crayon's point, attach a color-coordinated ribbon to look like a line of color.
6. If desired, use a real crayon to decorate a part of the top of the package to write a message to the recipient.

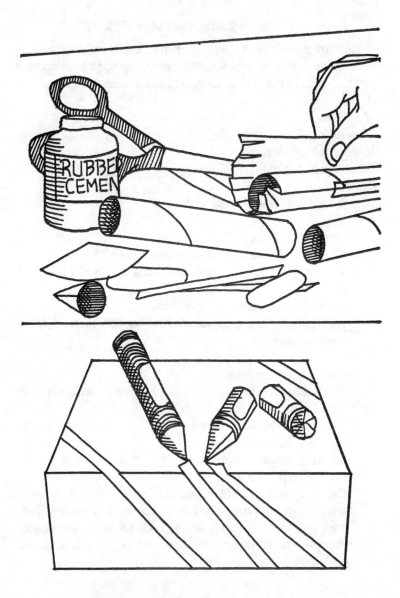

Constructing Colored Crayons over cardboard tubes.

Two Record Albums (Color Plate 6)

Here are a few ways to disguise record albums given as presents —put them in a specially decorated box; wrap them with another present; or make use of their shape and add a humorous touch.

Materials:
Glue stick
½-inch wide black ribbon
Construction paper
Glitter
½-inch wide double-stick tape

To make the Musical Staff Package:
1. Wrap the package normally in white paper.
2. Use the glue stick to "draw" the G clef and five lines for the staff.
3. Cover the glue lines with black ribbon.
4. Add musical notes, cut either from ribbon or from black construction paper.

To make the Glitter Package:
1. Wrap the package normally. Here, glittery silver paper is used.
2. Use the double-stick tape to write out the words, "Guess What's in Here."
3. Spread newspaper out on the work surface and place the package, tape side up, on it.
4. Gently sprinkle the glitter over the top of the package, covering the double-stick tape. After the tape is entirely covered, pick up the package and sprinkle off all the excess glitter onto the newspaper, so that you can return it to the container.

(Right) Decorating two record albums. Double-stick tape or glue provides the anchor for assorted decorations.

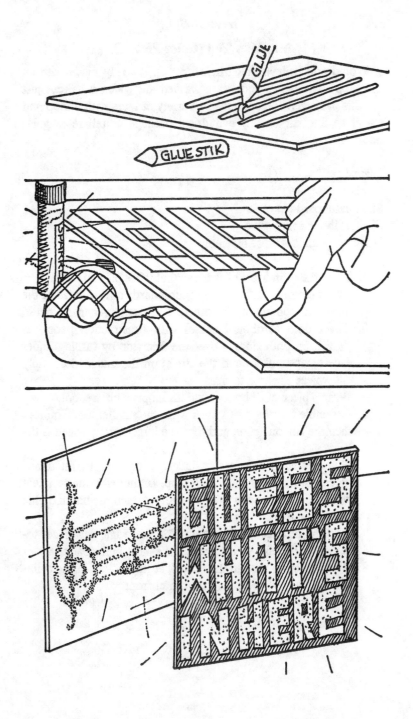

Mr. Mop Top (Color Plate 6)

Would you believe that Mr. Mop Top is really made with an old mop? The mop's ends were washed and given a haircut just for this package. You can make a variety of faces with a mop and use it as the hair on any cylindrical package or tall rectangular one.

Materials:
Mop
Shirt cardboard
Plastic ribbon spool
Novelty eyeglasses/nose assembly

1. Wrap the cylindrical package so that it has pleated ends.
2. Cut two circles from the shirt cardboard: one, the size of the plastic ribbon spool; the other, 2 inches larger in diameter.
3. Cover both cardboard circles with construction paper, as shown, on both sides. Cover the first side by turning under excess paper all around the circle; on the underside, simply cut a piece of paper to size.
4. Wrap a piece of ribbon around the empty ribbon spool.
5. Assemble the "hat" as shown, with the smaller circle on top, then the ribbon spool, and then the larger circle, which is the brim.
6. Glue the mop over the cylinder, using the glue at a few places on the sides—not on the top. (Otherwise, the recipient won't be able to open the package!) Attach the hat and glue it over the mop.
7. Add the novelty eyeglasses, and tie the frame ear pieces together (if necessary) underneath the mop, in the back.
8. Wrap a ribbon around the "neck" at the bottom of the cylinder. Add a bow tie here, at the center front.

Construction of Mr. Mop Top. Be certain not to put too much glue on the top, which would make the package difficult to open.

Piano Package (Color Plate 6)

This is a handsome wrapping for anyone interested in the piano —a singer, a voice coach, a pianist, an accompanist, etc. It makes use of a unique wrapping paper—sheet music.

Materials:
Sheet music
Black and white construction or gift wrapping paper
Black marker
Red ribbons

1. Wrap the package with sheet music, as you normally would.
2. Measure the top of the package and cut a rectangle of black paper to that size. Cut off 2 inches at one end to create the keyboard, as shown. Add a piece of white paper at that place, in its stead. Cut the black paper with a curve, to look like the top of a grand piano.
3. Use a ruler and the black marker to draw the keyboard on the piano.
4. Repeat the piano shape on newspaper, only this time making it significantly smaller, to fit on top of the first piano. When you have a suitable pattern, use it to cut out a piano shape from the sheet music. Then cut a slightly smaller one from solid black paper. Draw another keyboard on the smaller piano and attach both to the top of the first, as shown.
5. Decorate with red ribbons and looped bows.

"Cherry Tomato" or "Strawberry" Package (Color Plate 7)

This packaging for a bottle of wine makes use of a very commonplace item found at your local supermarket. Usually cherry tomatoes or strawberries come in small green plastic containers that look like tiny woven baskets. This bottle of wine, as pictured, looks like a growing strawberry itself, with all the red dotted paper and pretty leaves and flowers.

Materials:
Green plastic fruit basket
Green fabric or construction paper

1. Line the basket with the selected tissue paper.
2. Wrap the bottle in the same tissue paper and tie a cord around the neck, as shown, to gather a little excess paper there. Trim the paper so that it doesn't entirely envelop the bottle.
3. Insert the bottle into the plastic basket. Add extra paper all around the bottle to cushion and further decorate it.
4. Make small leaves from green fabric or paper and attach them at intervals around the bottle and at the neck. Add tiny novelty flowers.
5. Weave a white ribbon around the basket and tie a bow at the front center.

Magical Spaceship (Color Plate 7)

What child wouldn't want to receive a gift in this dazzling package!? After the present has been removed from the wrapping, the spaceship can be used over and over again for play, for toting lunches to school, or for another gift.

Materials:

Oatmeal container (or similar round container—the size you use determines the size of the gift you can put inside it)
Aluminum foil or silver gift wrapping paper
Shirt cardboard
Metallic ribbons, trims
Household items like bolts, "bubble" packaging wrap
Novelty American flag

1. Cover the exterior of the round container with aluminum foil or silver wrapping paper. If you cover it with foil, cut the piece exactly to size, to accommodate the height of the container. If you use silver gift wrapping paper, allow for a margin at the top, to turn into the inside of the package, and a margin on the bottom, to turn under to the bottom of the package, where you should make a pleated finish.

2. Make a "nose cone" for the top of the spaceship, as shown, from a triangular piece of cardboard. Notch the bottom edge to fit over the cardboard lid of the box.

3. Cover the nose cone with the same paper that is on the body of the rocket.

4. Use a decorative glittery ribbon and cover the edge of the nose cone on the rim of the lid.

5. Trim the bottom of the spaceship with a similar band of ribbon.

6. On the face of the body of the rocket, trim as desired, using whatever household objects you'd like to incorporate into the design.

7. Punch holes on each side of the rocket and feed a silvery cord through the holes to act as the carrier. Make a knot on the inside of the rocket to keep the cord in place.

8. Attach a small American flag to the top of the rocket.

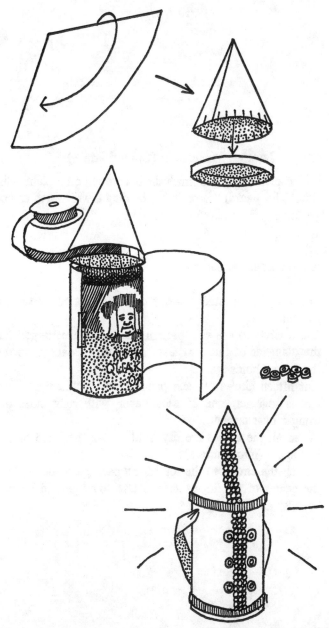

Construction of the Magical Spaceship. *Aluminum foil or silver gift wrapping paper makes this package very special and imperial-looking, but the use of everyday objects underscores just how easy it is to make.*

Jeweled Mushroom (Color Plate 8)

This is a splendid way to finish the decorating on a plain cylindrical box. This package is probably holding a wristwatch or bottle of perfume.

Materials:
Two color-coordinated papers

1. Wrap the box normally, with pleated finishes on the top and bottom.
2. Cut a circle to use as a pattern that is 4 inches larger than the diameter of the box. Use cardboard or oaktag, so that the pattern holds up.
3. Cut fifteen circles of each paper selected. "Laminate" two circles together, one of each paper, with right sides out, using rubber cement.
4. When all the circles are dry, fold each in half and then in half again (into quarters).
5. Attach the circles to the top of the package, radiating from the center of the lid, as shown. Use some glue in between "petals" as necessary.

Making the faceted components of the Jeweled Mushroom.

Bird in the Basket (Color Plate 10)

This package presents a few wrapping ideas in one design. The body of the bird shows how plain yarn can be used to wrap a round package (as mentioned in Chapter Three). The pattern for the Cone-shaped Box (in Chapter Four) can be used to make the bird's beak, enlarged or smaller, as desired. If you have a small gift you want to present in the cone-shaped box, you might make that box for the present and then use a Styrofoam ball to make the body of the bird, as shown here.

Materials:
1 Styrofoam ball, 6 inches in diameter
2 packages (approximately 10 yards) of wide yellow craft yarn
Novelty feathers
2 Novelty eyes

1. Make the cone-shaped box to the desired size, as instructed in Chapter Four. Here, orange paper is used for the outside of the package.
2. Carefully *pin* the cone-shaped box (beak) to the Styrofoam ball, so that the present can be removed from it and the bird put back together.
3. After the beak is attached, wrap the Styrofoam ball with the yellow yarn, beginning at the beak and working your way back to the other end, as shown. Use a little rubber cement, as necessary, to hold the yarn in place as you approach the opposite end.
4. Attach feathers and eyes to the front of the bird, adjacent to the beak.

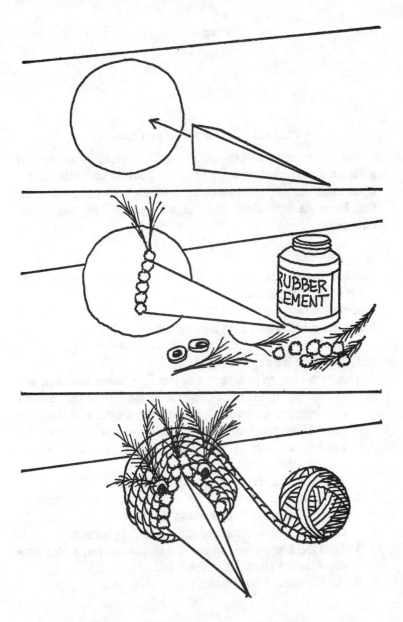

Constructing the body of a bird, using yarn wrapped around a Styrofoam ball for the base of the body.

Umbrella Package (Color Plate 11)

The classic umbrella box can be used to conceal other types of gifts; or, as expected, it can be used to hold an umbrella. In the latter case, you might design an umbrella right on the front of the box. Here, the umbrella is made three-dimensional by using a posterboard.

Materials:

Cardboard inner core from a roll of paper toweling (several cores for a long umbrella stem)

Posterboard

1 Styrofoam ball with a 1- to 2-inch diameter

1. Wrap the package normally.
2. Attach cardboard inner cores from the paper toweling, end to end, taping them together. Cover the top, at the handle's end, with color-coordinated paper. Do the same at the other end. (If only one cardboard tube is available, then cut off a small 1- to 2-inch section to use as the bottom end. Use the larger section for the handle.)
3. Attach the handle and bottom tip with glue.
4. To make the umbrella section, cut the pattern shape as shown and score lightly along the lines to make umbrella folds. Fold the posterboard and attach it to the box.
5. Glue the bottom section and the Styrofoam ball to the handle. Attach a gift tag, if desired.
6. Add decorative bows and ribbons, as desired.

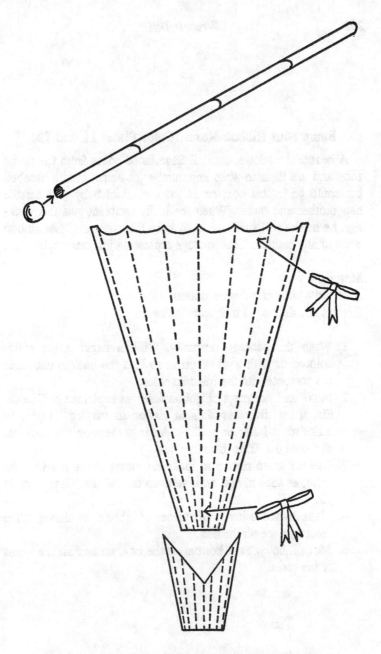

Follow the diagram for folding the umbrella shape. This form can be made in any size to accommodate your package.

Sumptuous Ribbon Roses (Color Plates 11 and 12)

A beautiful package, indeed! Save those boxes from the florist shop and use them to wrap any number of items—even a baseball bat could go in this box, or an assortment of baby gifts for the new mother and father. When the lucky recipient gets this package, he or she will surely want to keep this wrapping. Use ribbon roses in any fashion. This package represents just one application.

Materials:
Assorted widths of red satin ribbon
Green satin ribbon, ¼ inch wide for stems

1. Wrap the package normally, using a paper either solid-colored or with a small print, so that the background does not compete with the splendid roses.
2. Make an assortment of ribbon roses, as explained in Chapter Six, using diverse widths of ribbon in varying lengths, to make roses fuller or budlike. Arrange them on the package, as a bouquet. Glue them in place.
3. Use the green ribbon to make the stems of the roses. Twist them, as shown, and arrange them on the box. Glue them in place.
4. Make leaves using small pieces of ribbon, as shown. Glue them in place on the box.
5. Make a bow at the bottom of the box, around all the stems of the roses.

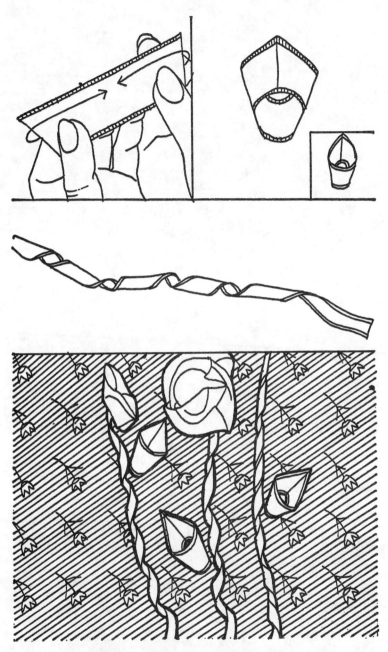

Construction of the ribbon roses, leaves, and stems for the
Sumptuous Ribbon Roses Package.